CULTIVATING LOVE

In a Culture Overgrown with Lust

Keith Brandon Sobus

PublishAmerica
Baltimore

First printing

PublishAmerica has allowed this work to remain exactly as the author intended, verbatim, without editorial input.

ISBN: 1-60610-288-5
PUBLISHED BY PUBLISHAMERICA, LLLP
www.publishamerica.com
Baltimore

Printed in the United States of America

Acknowledgments

(in no specific order)

Hannah Puffer, for her wonderful encouragement and for being my motivation for writing this book.

Raphael Francis and Stephen Maouyo for being great friends with great moral character which gave me hope when I needed it.

Joyce Sobus for being my Mom and holding me to a higher standard and raising me better than I could've ever asked.

Bob Sobus for being my Dad and being proud of everything I do, even for the seemingly insignificant things that I myself don't take pride in.

Ethan Magness of Mountain Christian Church for giving me his time and providing helpful criticism.

Bill and Lois of Forge Road Bible Chapel for their concern, wisdom, and quick response when I needed last minute criticisms before I turned in my final book.

Mark Moyer for being my Young Life leader and asking questions that I didn't want to confront.

Table of Contents

Part I

Introduction 9
Modern Culture 16
Wisdom 24
Love 33
Selfishness 44
Jealousy Is Evil 50
Submission 58
Understanding 70
Trust 79
Children and Parents 82

Part II

Responsibilities and Behaviors of a Boyfriend 93
"Checking Out" Girls and Flirting 95
Cheating 108
Pornography 120
Sex 130
Don't Date? 141
Masturbation 148
Drug Abuse 155
Too Late? 164
Goodbye 170
Notes 173

Part I

Introduction

My name's Keith. I try not to waste words, so this book should contain a lot of information in fewer pages, which is good, because if you're anything like me then you don't like to read a lot. I started writing this book when I was eighteen. It took me eighteen years to realize that my relationships could be more than they were. Then I realized I could help other people have better relationships by using what I learned. I also realized that you don't have to wait until you're eighteen to have great fulfilling relationships and I don't want people to have to make the same mistakes I made. So it's best to learn as early as possible, in my opinion.

High school was my biggest period of "enlightenment." My brother introduced me to his friend. His friend was twenty-something and was a leader for Young Life[1]. I was a freshman and couldn't understand why a twenty year old wanted to hang out with me. I didn't really mind though because not too many other people wanted to hang out with me quite as badly as he did (which isn't saying much). But that's a little off topic. Young Life is an international Christian organization, devoted to bringing kids to a personal relationship with God. And it was through Young Life and through conversations with my leader that I finally realized I could be having better relationships with girls that I was dating. I eventually became a leader myself a few months ago. The reason I'm telling you this is because it will come into play later.

I want you to know that this book only contains what I find to be true. I didn't write about things that I thought you'd want to hear. I didn't write this to make money by selling a book about things I thought people would like to hear. This book isn't made to help people feel better about what they've done or what they're doing. If I just wrote things you wanted to hear, it would be of no help to you, it wouldn't be sincere, and it would be a waste of your time.

Where to start...first of all, there are a lot of things I wish I had known sooner in life. The way I feel about it is, there is no excuse to not know these things sooner. The things I wish I had known and the wisdom I wish I had learned would've helped me make better decisions in life. I suppose that's why I feel the need to write this book. So that young men, and perhaps even older men and anybody else in between that hasn't had the chance to hear what I've heard and learn what I learned can get the opportunity to.

Hopefully the words and ideas contained in this book will shed some much needed light. Hopefully this book provides the insight that I was missing in my life before. I want to give to others what I would've liked to have had. These answers for how to create fulfilling relationships are hidden in the world. All we see and all we are bombarded by is how to have selfish, spur of the moment, passionate, meaningless, temporary relationships. This isn't how we were designed; it's not how our relationships are supposed to work.

The purpose of this book is to encourage the growth of strong loving relationships and allow young men to take pride in the relationships they build and take pride in their actions and the values which they uphold.

I also hope that in writing this book young women will be able to gain valuable insight. Young women should know what to expect from the boys they date. They should know that "the perfect guy" they're looking for is out there or at least a guy perfect enough to treat them like princesses (which will be addressed later).They should know they shouldn't have to settle. So many times I hear so many girls with absolute thoughts on men. "All men are liars, all men are cheats, all men check other girls out, all men flirt with other girls" and so on. This isn't true. It's half true, because certainly there are a lot of guys like that. If there weren't, I wouldn't feel the need to write this book.

So I do not blame girls for these thoughts. I blame us men, myself included; we have given girls the illusion that all men are terrible. When in reality, there are a few men out there who aren't all that bad. So we should take it upon ourselves to correct this misunderstanding. The only way to do this is for a change in behavior, which simply stems from a change in knowledge and then motivation to change. But motivation shouldn't be hard to find when it comes to relationships. Who would say "I think I'd like to have a less fulfilling relationship than possible." It doesn't seem like something a healthy minded person would say.

The words of this book will mostly be directed towards young Christian men, only because it makes things easier than being generically friendly and saying boy/girl all the time, and because I am a young Christian man and therefore have more grounds to advise young Christian men on their behavior than I would advising a woman on hers or an atheist on his. Christian beliefs and values were used not only because I am Christian but because I know that non-Christians can also find wisdom in the text of the bible regardless of whether or not they believe the stories to be true. I never could've written this book without God. So God must be given credit for it. I can't pretend like I could've been a good boyfriend or that I could've understood what it even meant to be a good boyfriend if it wasn't for God.

You do not have to be Christian in order to benefit from the words of the bible; surely we could all agree that it contains valuable lessons. Therefore everyone can learn from this book, regardless of religion, don't get me wrong though I will use plenty of pieces of reasoning and logic to back up my claims besides just the words of the bible. As a matter of fact this book shouldn't be read just by young Christian men, I everyone and anyone who is involved in relationships and who has an open mind should read this book, because everyone deserves to be happy and everyone owes it to themselves and their girlfriends to learn whether or not there are better ways to have relationships.

Secondly, some parts of this book may perhaps even end up being purposefully directed towards women and non-Christians, perhaps because what is directed to them is not necessary for men to hear, or Christians to hear. Just wanted to point that out because I realize I will not always be talking to Christian men, and I did not want to mislead anyone or have someone feel as if they were lied to about the motives of this book.

So here's what you can expect to read about in this book: a whole grocery list of ideas from love to sex to masturbation to porn to respect to flirting to romance and hopefully everything else in between. Some of it will most likely be a little controversial and most of it should cause you to think carefully and perhaps even reconsider how you do things. I hope it will be life changing for some of you and for others maybe it will reinforce what you've been thinking all along. However, even if all this book did was give people more understanding of why certain people chose to live the way they do, I would be more than happy. My main goal is to provide information on subjects that people don't normally talk about but also I'd love to see people make wise decisions about their relationships. Mostly because I don't like to see girls mistreated.

The next chapter will discuss modern culture and will take a look at what messages the world is trying to send us.

The following two chapters afterwards will define wisdom and love. Both are words that can mean different things to different people and so it is important that to define wisdom and love so that you will know what I mean when I use those words throughout this book.

The following chapters after Modern Culture, Wisdom, and Love don't need to be read in chronological order. Rather, read what you would like to know most about, read what you are most interested in first. The chapters that don't interest you shouldn't be disregarded because they will be filled with helpful, relative, and unexpected information, so be sure to read those too.

Modern Culture

I feel like it's important to address modern culture, as it exists in America, I can't say much about other countries because I am not well experienced in their culture. However, it's obvious that part of American culture is largely based on sex and probably safe to assume that the same goes for most countries.

A lot of American culture would have you think that sex is casual, has no ramifications and should be explored in a variety of ways. You may disagree or find this information to be a bit harsh, but give me a chance to explain my reasoning and perhaps you may come to agree. If you've ever watched the popular television sitcom, "Friends", it wouldn't take you long to realize that these people had sex all the time with close friends and even strangers. It was never once addressed in the episodes that there was anything wrong with this lifestyle. None of their sexual behavior had ramifications, thus leading to the unhealthy view that sex has no consequences.

If you've ever watched HBO's Sex and the City you'd soon learn that it's exactly what it sounds like it'd be about. Women seek happiness through sex in almost every episode. The writers act like its great, the actors act like its great, the viewers act like it's great. American society accepts the notion that sex should be casual.

Cosmopolitan magazines print headlines such as "Our New Sex Position 77, it's as mind blowing as that other number", "20 Sexifiers", "How to Turn Him on Without Touching", "How to Truly Surprise a Man in Bed", "Erotic Sex, 7 Boundary Pushing Moves", and "30 Sex Boosters." All I did to find these headlines was type cosmopolitan magazine in Google images and the first few covers that came up boasted such headlines. Don't we see a problem with this? Don't you feel like there are some things you and your partner are supposed to discover together? Don't you think some things are sacred and personal and you shouldn't be learning them from magazine covers? Don't you see that this tells young girls what their lives need to be like in order to be happy? Don't you see the deception?

Even Seventeen magazine, read by middle school

girls and high school girls all over the nation has headlines written by adults that say things like "405 Ways to Look Hot at Every Party", "Are You Sure You're Still a Virgin?", "The Best Jeans For Your Butt", "Get a Nice Bikini Butt", "Exclusive Survey, Sex, Love, and Teens", and "Should You Make the First Move." All point towards sexual indiscretion. All show teenagers that in order to get attention, in order to be popular, in order to fit in and be like the girls on the covers of the magazines, making millions a year, they need to focus on sex. They need to show off their bodies. It's all bullshit and it should be just as passionately upsetting for everyone. Not just I, not just a 19 year old boy, but to adults, even the ones who write that trash.

But how about Cosmo Girl "The ultimate teen site for games, beauty, fashion...and more!" what do those magazines have to say to our thirteen year olds who they so proudly call out to on their websites with promises of games, beauty and fashion? With a cover of Paris Hilton, the perfect role model for all our teens (sarcasm) we see headlines like "10 Ways to Turn Guys On (Without Taking Clothes Off!)", or other covers that boast "Guys Talk Sex! What his X-Rated Requests Really Mean", or "Blow His Mind! The trick that'll have him aching for you." Why would we allow our loved ones to become consumed in such filth? To have their minds manipulated at such an early age, telling them that this is how life needs to work? What else are they supposed to think when it's all around them? Am I suggesting for us to not read these types of magazines? Yes. Am I suggesting that if we have kids we shouldn't let them read these magazines? Yes, most definitely.

It isn't just this way for girls but for boys too. Every time we see a music video, men are treating women like objects that are purely there for sexual enjoyment. There's nothing "cool" about commitment in today's society. Whose fault is it? It's the adults, the people who set the standards. The people in charge of music, in charge of raising children, in charge of publishing magazines and making movies and writers of television shows, it's their fault. It's our fault.

Either the authors and publishers have sold their soul for their greed and love of money or they truly believe in what they're writing. Sitcom writers, soap opera writers, movie script writers, they all either sell their soul and make infidelity look romantic and passionate, and make being sexually active seem like it's the right thing to do in order to make a few bucks or they really do believe it. Either way, it's just as bad.

You see, sex sells. If people were to actually come out and say that sex is a gift and should be kept sacred and personal, then people would have to figure out a new way to sell their items. Who would want to do that? Certainly not upstanding adults with strong moral fiber, no they'd much rather corrupt and manipulate vulnerable children.

I can't help but think that all of these adults should realize that no matter how much you have sex in how many different positions wearing how many different pieces of lingerie, with however many people, sex is still unfulfilling for them. I can't believe it. It seems to me like every once in a while they'd end up having to take a serious look at things and be extremely honest with themselves and just admit that they weren't happy. It's hard for me to imagine why they'd bring down their children's generation and make them suffer the same fate that they've put themselves through. And encourage such a lifestyle by writing magazine articles about how insignificant sex is.

So how has all of this impacted or culture? Is it impacting our culture? Is it really adding up to any significant amount of damage? Are kids increasingly more sexual, and more sexually disturbed?

Let's look at some disturbing facts. Thirty-one percent of young women become pregnant at least once before they reach the age of 20—about 750,000 a year. Eight in ten of these pregnancies are unintended and 81 percent are to unmarried teens. The United States has the highest rates of teen pregnancy and births in the western industrialized world. Eight in ten girls and six in ten boys say they wish they had waited until they were older to have sex. These facts come from: http://www.teenpregnancy.org/ resources/data/national.asp

http://www.guttmacher.org/pubs/fb_ATSRH.html ("The Guttmacher Institute advances sexual and reproductive health worldwide through an interrelated program of social science research, public education and policy analysis.") reports Nearly half (46%) of all 15-19-year-olds in the United States have had sex at least once. By age 15, 13% of teens have ever had sex. However, by the time they reach age 19, seven in 10 teens have engaged in sexual intercourse. Eleven percent of all U.S. births are by teens.

Maybe statistics aren't enough to truly hit home. One of the best men I know, and a great friend of mine, works at a restaurant as a waiter. He went into work one day not long ago and overheard a conversation that another waiter was having. This coworker was bragging about how he had gone to a "swingers" party. He was invited by a girl at a table that he waited on. It's bad enough that this guy had a girlfriend but a "swingers" party is a horrid, perverse thing. I won't get into the details but needless to say he continued to brag about how he had sex with other people's wives. And what makes it even worse is that a good amount of the guys in the conversation were encouraging him and telling him how jealous they were that he got to go. Is something wrong with our society that people come to think like this?

Of course that's just one personal experience that was handed down by word of mouth. You could always go online and see for yourself how many newspaper articles are written about high school and middle school students having sex in school and their friends are commenting on how it's not a big deal. Furthermore you could find newspaper articles on high school students having orgies and how their parents provided houses and may have even engaged in the sexual acts.

Hopefully you're either disgusted, angry, or in complete disbelief by now. But needless to say, things need to change.

In the chapters to come a different way of life will be discussed; one that focuses on commitment and relationships and everlasting love and romance and passionate, real sex. Because not all sex is bad, as a matter of fact it can be the greatest thing you've ever experienced, but only if it happens in the way it was intended to happen.

Wisdom

Wisdom, as defined by the American Heritage Dictionary (according to dictionary.com) is, "The ability to discern or judge what is true, right, or lasting; insight." So, we can see why wisdom would be good to have when forming good, lasting relationships. But to elaborate on the definition of wisdom, I would say that wisdom is the opposite of foolishness. Wisdom is what separates men from children. Everyone is capable of being wise. It is not something that certain people are more gifted at than others. Maybe that's the beauty of it. Wisdom is learning life's true lessons and applying it to your life. There is only benefit to being wise. There is no benefit to being foolish. Ecclesiastes 10:1, "As dead flies give perfume a bad smell, so a little folly outweighs wisdom and honor." They say ignorance is bliss, but ignorance is just the illusion of bliss, the closest we can ever get to bliss is to having a righteous life, gained through knowledge and wisdom, not the opposite. Ecclesiastes also tells us in chapter 7 verse 19 that, "One wise person is stronger than ten leading citizens of a town!" Now, another way to say this is that a foolish man is still a child while I was child is truly a man. Which is sad because generally when people talk about "who is a man and who isn't" they generally base it off of who has had the most sex. For instance, I sat around a room with my friend's Dad and some of his Dad's friends. Everyone was joking around and I noticed that only one of them wasn't smoking so I asked him if he was a girl (Of course, I was kidding.) But after I said that he sat back and laughed. Then, in order to prove that he was a man his friend took over and began to brag about how much sex this guy had and how many different girls he had slept with. The only thing I kept trying to figure out was, why would this make anyone a man? How does our culture not teach this man to be embarrassed of his lifestyle? Morals make someone a man. Wisdom makes someone a man. Random sex does not make anyone a man and the Sex chapter will explain that more.

But that isn't just one random occasion. Everyone has heard someone exclaim "Hey, you're finally a man." when they're talking to someone who has lost their virginity for the first time. In one form or another, this phrase is used commonly throughout the world. And what we should be asking is "How in the heck did our culture adopt the belief that sex made you a man?" Anyone can have sex but it is much harder for people to have high moral standards.

Wisdom is something gained through experience. However we do not have to experience things ourselves to gain wisdom. We don't have to have sex with tons of people before learning that it's unsatisfying and deciding we would've been better off having sex with just one person. We can learn from the experience of others. That is one of life's true lessons. Some things should not be experienced. We do not have to go through the trouble of adding pain and sorrow and remorse to our lives in order to gain wisdom. Although you can gain firsthand knowledge of a subject, it is not always beneficial to. Some things are better to learn from the misfortune of others than from your own misfortune.

This one time, my friend, who will be called Kate to protect her privacy and our confidentiality, was hanging out with me in the parking lot of her school. It was midnight and we had nothing to do so we ended up having a random deep conversation. She began asking me questions "Why don't you do drugs? Why don't you cheat? Why do you live so conservatively, why not get in more trouble?" Not because she was judging me but just out of friendly conversation, she wanted to know my side of the story. I didn't really have a good answer prepared and I'm pretty sure I just shrugged and said "Why not?" That's when she said, "We only live once." That was her reason. "We only live once so why not party it up and enjoy life and get wasted and enjoy lots of sex (or whatever your temptations are). In fact I've heard this phrase many times "We only live once." Every time I've heard it it's used to justify doing risky or dangerous things. I hear it used all the time, but it couldn't be more backwards. The truth is, we *do* only live once, and life *is* short. So even better that we do not screw up our only shot, our only chance at having a fulfilling life.

Their reasoning for maintaining the lifestyle that they have contradicts their very actions. Perhaps if we lived more than once we would have reason to screw up one of our lives. Perhaps than we could justify ruining our lives and giving into the temptations of sin since we would have an extra life for doing what is right. But please do not take your only life for granted. Do not waste it or ruin it.

Life on earth is, undisputedly, the greatest gift God has given us. Angels do not even get to experience what we have. We are very fortunate. We have the chance to face trials and temptations. We have the chance to gain wisdom and strength. We have the chance to test our limits and abilities. We have life, and with it, we have responsibility, the responsibility to use our lives and not waste our lives. Because we have been given a gift greater than anything we could possibly imagine. Now, for arguments sake, lets just say someone says, “Well, angels might not have it all that great either, who’s to say they don’t face trials and temptations?” I would say to them that that’s very true but angels don’t get the chance to believe in god and love him without seeing him, therefore life on earth is still the greatest gift.

For this reason we must try to make our lives easy, so that we can love our life and not take it for granted. Do not complicate yourselves, worrying about trivial matters that do not have significance. If you get lost, know that it is not the end of the world. If you get stuck behind a slow driver, know that it is not the end of the world. If a driver bumps into your BMW, know that your BMW is not important. If you can’t afford a car, know that cars aren't everything. Know that your happiness is what matters. Know that you still have life and therefore, you have nothing to complain about. I won't pretend that this applies to everyone, but generally, if you have picked up this book and are reading it, it probably applies to you.

One of my favorite quotes is, "It's all small stuff." Which pretty much implies, don't sweat the small stuff, oh and by the way, it's all small stuff. The reason I love this quote so much is that it just points out how insignificant our problems are compared to the grandiose universe we live in. Yep...grandiose.

Sure, life has its ups and down. More often than not, it has its downs. But we have the ability to limit these "downs" we have the ability to limit them for ourselves and for others. So why not make life easy for yourself and take it for what it is. Do not take it for granted. At the very least, know that these pitfalls of life add to our lives. Remind yourselves constantly that if we had nothing wrong in the world, no sadness, no pain, no sorrow; remind yourselves that life would be boring. Remind yourselves that we would not know what happiness was without experiencing sorrow.

Learn to love your life. Learn to not take your life for granted; in order to love others you must be able to love yourself. And you must seek wisdom. Wisdom will help you love yourself and will show you the way to loving others. Seeking wisdom is also a sign that you are trying to love yourself. “He who gets wisdom loves his own soul; he who cherishes understanding prospers.” Proverbs 19:8[3]

Many people find it easier to not challenge or think about their morals. Many people find it easier to not think about whether or not how they’re living is wrong. I believe part of this is fear that they will regret something they did in their past or simply they fear that they will have to change and they just aren’t ready to make that step yet.

People always say “live with no regrets.” They generally mean that you should never dwell on or think about things in the past, or at least should never regret anything that you do. Well, I’ll touch on some of this later but I’d like to leave you with the thought that if you live a righteous way and minimize the amount of things that you might regret, it will be much easier to “live with no regrets.” After all, having nothing to regret in the first place is much better than having things to regret but just deciding that you don’t care about those things because you want to be as happy as you can and that means ignoring pain that you’ve caused yourself and others.

This would be a good time to talk about relationships. Many people will continue dating people even if they know they don't want to marry their partner. I have met many people, just looking for a "summer fling." Or simply people who date because they like the initial feeling of having a crush on someone, they crave the "butterflies in the stomach" feeling. It's kind of immature and foolish to feel this way, to invest so much time and emotion in something so temporary. Sure you gain experience and make memories with people. But some of these memories are things that you should be making for the first time with your husband, or with someone who you will love, someone who is worth it. Why would you waste the time dating someone who won't appreciate you or who you won't appreciate? It is a selfish and foolish thing to do; to live for the moment and not think about the future, to not think about how you could be affecting your future relationships. What you're doing is creating memories that have no context and value in your life. You're doing things that will "taint" your love and your meaningful relationships.

It is so frustrating for me to think about the people in my life who I have seen make these same mistakes and to regret it afterward. And men, it is expected of you to treat women the way you would want someone to treat your future wife. It is expected of you to treat women the way you want your daughter to be treated. It is expected of you to treat your sisters or your friends in a way to show them that they deserve respect from other men and that they are people to be valued and treated with dignity. If you are mean to your sister, will she not expect most men to be mean?; if you treat your female friends as if they are sexual objects will they not expect most men to treat them as sexual objects? But what if you treat your sister with love and show her that she is to be respected and treated with dignity? Then when she meets a man who isn't fit to be her husband, she won't think she must settle with him, she will have higher expectations, and therefore a much more fulfilling relationship. If you treat your friends with respect and dignity will they not also look for other men in their lives who will do the same?

Like I said before, wisdom will help you love yourself and will show you the way to loving others. Well, now that you all have the gist of what I mean when I speak of "wisdom" perhaps it is time to move on to love.

Love

The importance of defining love is so that you understand what is meant when you see the word "love". This is strictly my definition of love, in my own terms, you may have your own thoughts of love or even your own definition, but when the word "love" appears in this book, you will understand what is mean by it. Unfortunately love has been defined so differently by everybody on the face of the earth that some of the feelings and meanings evoked by love have been diminished and warped. It has been used as a very vague term that's open to interpretation. Everybody has their own definition of love. Most often than not, their definition tends to demean the true, pure, essence of love. For example, popular lyrics for a song are "those three words are not enough."[1] Three words meaning "I love you." The very fact of the matter is, those three words can be enough. They are enough. But the songwriter's definition of love may not be as strong as it should be. If he had held love in a higher esteem he never would've said that. He would've known that those three words are huge, those three words work miracles, those three words are the greatest thing you could ever tell anybody. Or at least they can be, if you see them that way. And who would choose to diminish the value of their own love? It's a pretty foolish thing to do. That's important to reiterate: You have the chance to establish the value of your own love and you have the ability to make it so that, when you say "I love you" to someone, it will have enough power and enough meaning behind it to make someone cry with joy. Or, you can demean the value of your love so that when you tell someone you love them, it would be no different then saying you love nachos. I have a good friend who I envy in a lot of ways. He told me that he wasn't going to say "love" until he was married. That's exactly what I'm talking about. When he says "love" it will carry much more meaning then when I say "love." I envy it.

And then at the other end of the spectrum, I've seen the word "love" used too liberally. I had a friend tell me she loved a boy. Meanwhile she managed to make out with other boys. I had a friend tell me he was in love, soon after that he broke up with his girlfriend because his parents didn't want him to date her. I've had a teacher tell the class that to believe in love is naive. Well, the girl who was "in love" wasn't really in love, not the kind of love I talk about, because if she was, she never would've wanted to hurt the boy at all, and kissing other boys would certainly do the trick. After all, how could we ever willingly hurt the ones we loved with such selfishness? Surely this cannot be love. And moreover, if she was in love, shouldn't she have been able to resist the temptation to casually make out with people? Who could ever take her seriously if she told people she loved them? She has demeaned and diminished the value of her love.

The boy who loved his girlfriend but then left her because his parents said he had to. Was this love? No. If you can't fight for your love, chances are, it is not love. I heard in a movie once, a man said... anything in this world that's worth having, must be worth fighting for. I think love falls under this category. Now, don't get me wrong you should always respect your parents, however if you really were in love, then its time to be a man and make decisions on your own. This boy has diminished the value of his love, because he has shown other people that when he says love, he doesn't mean the sort of love where you would do anything you could to be with a person. He really means, I like you to an extent, but I would never date you if my parents asked me not to.

And finally, for the teacher, there are many reasons why he may not believe in love, and we'll get to them later. But the thing that got me most was how in the exact sentence following that, he stated that a father once ran a triathlon with his handicapped son, carrying him along the way. And that his father was a true hero. Now this isn't the romantic love that I'm talking about, but it's certainly a part of romantic love. That is how we should love our girlfriends. That is love. Love is a huge driving power which causes ordinary men to do extraordinary things. We cannot overlook it and we cannot take it for granted because it is a great gift.

As a matter of fact, the second greatest gift we have been given is love. (Maybe… actually I haven't really made a list of God's gifts in order of greatness… but if I did, love would be somewhere at the top, along with life and wisdom. Also, I'm being pretty sarcastic at this moment; I think it's pretty lame to number gifts "in order of greatness")

There's something strange about love, we can't

know God if we don't know love because God is love and at the same time, in order to love fully, we must understand God's love, or understand the concept of God's love. You do not have to be a Christian to love. You do not have to be a believer of any religion to love. You do not have to be a romantic, and idealist, an optimist or a dreamer. A realist can love, a pessimist can love. You must only be wise to love. Love demands wisdom. To clear things up, back when I said that you can't know God unless you know love, what I meant was... that until you feel someone love you, until you feel appreciated by someone and loved to the full amount, then it's kind of hard to imagine why God would ever love you. So therefore, when you feel loved, you can finally believe, beyond a shadow of a doubt that God loves you. And once you've reached this part, then you can take your love to a higher level by understanding God.

Understand God. Even if you do not believe in God, you can make sense of what I have to say. You see, God knows everything about us, and still loves us. God knows all of our sins, all of our bad thoughts, and yet he still loves us. God knows how many times we've doubted him and he still loves us. God knows how many times we've blasphemed against him. He knows when we did wrong and when we didn't do right. But he still loves us. Would someone love you if they knew everything about you? Would you love someone even if you knew everything about them? Every time they've betrayed you with their hearts and minds. Would you still love them unconditionally like God would? This is the love we should strive for.

There is no greater feeling than to be loved. There is no greater thing than to have someone know everything about you and still love you. There is nothing better than waking up every day and knowing that you are loved for who you are.

We should not compete with God's love. We should not try to love better than God. But we should strive to love like God. Nothing is more beautiful than Gods love. If we want to care for our girlfriends, we must strive to love them with the love they deserve. We must strive for an untainted, immaculate love. After all, don't they deserve it? Don't you want what's best for the one you love?

Love demands wisdom, love demands forgiveness, love demands understanding, love demands sharing, love demands openness, love demands sacrifice, love demands you. You and your ability to give the word "love" the respect is deserves by giving it special meaning and not tossing it around loosely, but by acting on it when you say you love someone.

Love is the most progressive powerful force on the planet (I say progressive because there is always the force of evil which only destroys the world instead of improving upon it). Any time the world has been changed for the better, love has been the guiding force. Gandhi loved. Jesus loved. Martin Luther King loved. Missionaries love. Volunteers love. Love can overcome all things. Love is not bound by space, time, or even death. Love does not discriminate. The bible knows this great power of love; Songs of songs 8:7 says, "Many waters cannot quench love; rivers cannot wash it away. If one were to give all the wealth of his house for love, it would be utterly scorned."

Love is not bound by space. Love is not conquered by distance. People can love each other miles apart. People can love each other worlds apart. Love is not conquered by time. People can love each other for their entire lives. People can love each other from the time they meet until the time they die. Love is not conquered by death. It is possible to love someone long past the time of their death.

This is not to say that love has never faded. This

is not to say that love has never lost. Without wisdom, love can never last. Love can be strengthened and weakened. It is up to us to make the effort to not let our love become weak. If we have wisdom, we have the resources to keep our love strong. Strong enough to withstand any trials this world can throw at us. What more could we want?

You may be asking yourself, how does a realist believe in such things? How does a skeptic believe in such things, how could a pessimist love? Love does not discriminate. Anyone can love. A realist can believe in love, because love does happen. Many stories can be used as evidence to support the power of love. There is no doubt that people love and that it has had huge incomparable effects to this world. Love is a real thing. A skeptic can believe in such things, because he will eventually come across love. Perhaps he will not feel it himself, closing himself off from the possibility of love, but it is inevitable that he will see it in his lifetime. There are a multitude of examples of love that have lasted and not failed. A pessimist can believe in love, he may not believe he will ever find it, but eventually he could, and then when he did find it, he would believe. So there, love is for everyone.

I'd also like to say that love does not discriminate

over age. I think a child can love just as much as a man can, if he has enough wisdom. It's popular to hear "they're too young to be so serious." The truth is, you aren't too young to be so serious. Because like all things, love is a learning-experience and it is never too early to learn. And the truth is, love should be something to celebrate, love is not some sort of burden that young people shouldn't have to be bothered by. It is a joyous thing which people should rejoice in. Love is the second greatest gift God has given us, how can we take it away from children? Do they not also deserve God's gifts? It should be noted that it is widely accepted that Christ's' apostles were of high school age. If God felt them worthy to lead an entire religion, then I would think that he should be okay if they fell in love.

Now there's another thing interesting about love, it's not a necessity, and not only that but you don't have to be in love with someone if you don't want to be. You don't have to be in a bad, unhealthy relationship, you don't have to fall in love with the wrong person, and you don't have to leave your girlfriend for someone else, and you don't have to commit adultery.

Love is not out of our control. Now we certainly can't make ourselves love someone, for example if you pitied someone, you couldn't make yourself love him just because you wanted to, and it would be a bad and unhealthy relationship. But if you started to fall for someone that wasn't your girlfriend or that wouldn't be a good girlfriend for you, well, you have a choice to either fall in love with her or not. You don't have to feed your temptations and attractions. It may be more romantic to pretend like there was some invisible force that fate had created that was unstoppable and that you couldn't get away from. But that's not the case, and we are smart enough to know that. You are smart enough to realize that. No one ever falls in love with axe murderers or rapists or child molesters, this is because people have chosen to be disgusted by axe murderers and such. So you can choose to be disgusted with the thought of dating a girl that wasn't right for you or for breaking up with your girlfriend for someone you just met, or disgusted with the thought of cheating on your girlfriend. The point is, you have a choice and when an adult says "I cheated on my wife because I fell in love. I couldn't help it." They are being foolish and childish and just plain wrong. It's a cop out and it's a lie. And for you women, any man who isn't disgusted by adultery isn't a man worth dating and so If he cheats on his wife with you or leaves his girlfriend for you (and he just met you) then you shouldn't confuse his stupidity and think it's "romantic." It isn't its heartless and gutless. And I apologize for getting so worked up about it.

Now that we have a broad understanding of what I mean when I say love, we can begin to understand what the duties and responsibilities are that come with love.

SELFISHNESS

Being selfless is an important aspect in a relationship. If you are devoted to the growth of love, being selfless should be a priority. The word selfish comes up a lot in this book as being a bad thing. I'm aware that some people may not know what's wrong with only being concerned about their selves. So this chapter is an attempt to tackle this subject and explore the immorality of it.

I spent a lot of time online researching selfishness. There are a lot of websites that would have you believe you should be selfish whenever possible because it is the only way to be happy in life. It's a lie. It's another piece of evidence of how our modern culture is guiding people down the wrong path.

The Merriam-Webster Dictionary (found online) would define the word selfish as:

"**1:** concerned excessively or exclusively with oneself **:** seeking or concentrating on one's own advantage, pleasure, or well-being without regard for others **2:** arising from concern with one's own welfare or advantage in disregard of others"

It's an excellent place to start. "Concerned excessively of exclusively with oneself" implies that you just don't care about other people or you don't put other people's worth into consideration when you act. You could care less about other people. This is not a loving way to think. This doesn't bode well for relationships, and so when I point out different kinds of behavior that can be seen as selfishness, you should take it seriously into consideration and decide whether or not you feel a need to change.

You cannot possibly be in a loving relationship if one partner is determined to be selfish. Such a thing won't last. Relationships are about being selfless. Relationships are about sacrifice.

There's a whole philosophy called altruism. It's based on the selfless concern for other people's well being. It's based on putting other people's needs and wants before your own. Many people in opposition of altruism say that there is no way to survive, in theory. That's also a lie. Imagine if two people in a relationship behaved altruistically. Both would want the best for one another. None would cheat, none would make fun of the other or hurt the others feelings in some way, none would be neglected, none would be forced to do something he or she didn't want to do.

Somebody close to me once said "It is a man's right to fight for his freedom, but it is a man's responsibility to fight for his brother's freedom." In other words, my friend felt that if he was being stripped of freedom, then he had the right to fight for his freedom but if someone else was being stripped of their freedom, not only did he have the right to help him but he was obligated to. It's the notion that all people are united simply because we are human and we have a bond and we should be responsible enough to lift each other up and love each other and not hate and not fight and not work for personal gain, but work towards the gain of everybody.

People who work for charities and do volunteer work or missionary work, they are known to be people of love, they are known well for living their lives and helping when complete strangers were being neglected. Everyone in Africa helping the AIDS relief effort falls under this category. People who devote their time and lives to helping the mentally challenged, fall under the category of altruism. People who open up soup kitchens are altruistic.

To be selfish promotes the idea that you are the most important thing in the universe. I look at my life and think: there are other people who deserve food more than I do. There are better people than me who are starving. There are people being killed and hunted down by their government who have better morals than me. I look at my life and realize I don't deserve all the blessings I've been given. I know enough not to think that I am the center of the universe. I know enough not to think that I am owed something by anyone.

Let's picture a hypothetical world where selfishness was the ultimate and one true value. What would this world look like? People would kill each other just to be able to have their stuff. What if people had been continually selfish since the dawn of humanity? There'd be war and mass chaos. Raping women would be totally okay. Raping children would be okay too, as long as someone was doing it for their own personal gain. Don't we see how foolish it is to believe in selfishness?

How about a world where selflessness was the ultimate and one true value? It isn't that people would starve to death, trying to help others and never being helped themselves, it's that everyone would eat because everyone would be watching out for each other. Everyone would have shelter. If someone was sick they would be cared for. There'd be no war over someone else's land or oil, because you'd just share it. No one would have a need to get rich or store up money.

It's so simple to see that selfishness is not a good value to have. Sure, I took it to the extreme level, but sometimes taking things to the extreme helps to simplify whether or not they are right or wrong. Even on the moderate level, selfishness is wrong. Like knowing that you and your friend are equally thirsty and there is only one cup of water, so you race to it to be the first to drink it. When you could've just split it and it wasn't a big deal. It's wrong. Or you could've let him have it all, knowing it wouldn't be the end of the world.

Please, do not be selfish if you're in a committed relationship. It isn't fair to the other person. If you want to be selfish at least give the other person fair warning and don't deceive them about your notions of what is right and wrong.

I'm going to take selfishness an extra step further. There's a school of thought that all evil comes from pride. I think it would be a vast improvement to say that all evil comes from selfishness. I think pride is a form of selfishness. I can't think of a sin that doesn't tie into selfishness. I've seen websites promoting selfishness. Now I tell you that all evil stems from selfishness. It's funny to think that two completely different theories can come from the same planet. I'm surprised to think that someone could lead themselves to believe that selfishness is a good thing.

We hurt people for selfish reasons, we put ourselves above other people for selfish reasons, we murder for selfishness, we steal out of selfishness, we lie out of selfishness, and we sin because of selfishness. I challenge you to think of a sin where selfishness isn't a major aspect. Selfishness is a terrible thing. Strive to be selfless and you will find yourself happy.

Jealousy Is Evil

I don't really mean that jealousy is evil. I don't mean it at all. The world means it, and would tell you it if you asked or even if you didn't ask. The world hates jealousy. I'm not talking about envy. Envy is, wanting what you don't have. I'm talking about jealousy. I'm talking about being protective of what you already have and feeling a mix of anger and fear when you feel that what you have is being threatened. Why does the world hate jealousy? The world instills values of liberalism, relationships included. The world doesn't want relationships where each person owns each other and are committed to each other completely. The world wants free relationships where passion and pleasure are the focal point.

Swingers hate jealousy. A swinger cannot exist if he or she is jealous. Swingers do not believe that they belong to one another. They desecrate relationships and faithfulness. A liberal relationship longs to be free and maybe not to the extent of a swinger always, but along the same lines. If you flirt with the wife or girlfriend of someone in a liberal relationship, they will not care. If you "check out" a girlfriend or wife who is in a liberal relationship they will not care. They believe that they live for themselves and so they cannot expect their partner to think differently. So both partners mutually agree that they will only do what's beneficial for themselves and not for each other. Therefore why should they care if someone flirts with the other? They do not expect anyone not to, nor do they care at all because they do not own that person.

The prospect of owning another person seems terrible. People will say "I'm not an object." "I'm not anyone's slave." "I'm not a possession." But if you are in a loving committed relationship, than you will want to be the other persons slave. And that other person will want to be your slave. It isn't unfair. It's a mutual ownership. The ability to be able to say, "I'm all yours." and "You're all mine." It isn't horrible or evil to want this kind of relationship. It's loving. If a husband sees another man flirting with his wife, he should get jealous. He has a right to be jealous because only he has a right to flirt with his wife, only he has a right to "check out" his wife. This can be the same for relationships, depending on what standards you and your partner set for your relationship.

People will say, there's nothing loving about jealousy. Jealousy stems from insecurity. Sometimes it is true. More often than not however, it isn't about not trusting your partner. It isn't about thinking she will be unfaithful. It isn't about thinking that you're not good looking enough to be able to keep your girlfriend. It's about not wanting other people to get pleasure from your girlfriend in ways that they don't have the right to. I.e. flirting, checking out, touching, etc. If your girlfriend kissed another guy, you would get jealous, not because of insecurity but because the guy has no right to touch your girlfriend like that. It's okay to be protective of what you love. And so if a guy puts his arm around your girlfriend, than you also have the right to be jealous.

You should be protective of your lover. People often say, "Wouldn't you want what's best for your girlfriend, even if that means being with someone else?" That's a ridiculously absurd question. Of course you don't think she'd be better with someone else if you love her. Because you think you're meant to be with her, because you think you love her like no one else can, because you think you love her the way she deserves to be loved and you know no one else will give her the same respect and adoration and commitment. You should be possessive when it comes to not wanting to share your love.

Don't get me wrong jealousy can be overbearing, demanding, repulsive, hostile, even abusive and dangerous. That's not the kind of jealousy I'm talking about. Believe it or not, I'm talking about a Godly kind of jealousy, something that's rarely discussed outside of the Christian community, even rarely discussed inside the Christian community due to the influence of modern culture.

To some of you this will be brand new information. You see, in exodus, God declares that you should not praise or worship false idols, because God is a jealous God. God is talking about a zealous jealousness. They actually say that one of God's names is "Jealous." This is what we should strive for. What does it mean to be zealous? Merriam-Webster online dictionary describes zeal as "eagerness and ardent interest in pursuit of something." with synonyms of fervor and passion. Does this sound like love? Dictionary.com defines zeal as "fervor for a person, cause, or object; eager desire or endeavor; enthusiastic diligence; ardor."

Does this sound like love? So to have eager, diligent, passionate desires to protect, keep and love something that only you should have, is there anything wrong with that? Is there anything wrong with wanting to keep something that is precious to you? No there is isn't. If you hold something near and dear to your heart than how could someone translate that as being evil?

If the person you're dating gets jealous because a girl flirted with you, don't be upset, don't get defensive. Talk things out. Realize that she loves you and that she is being jealous out of love, as long as it's the kind of love described above. On the other hand, if someone is being jealous for seemingly ridiculous reasons than try to have a conversation with them, not an argument. Talk things out, explain the situation, and keep in mind their view of everything. The least you could do is understand their concerns and try to put them to ease. Most of the time, when people are expressing jealousy, they are simply looking for reassurance. If there isn't anything for them to get jealous about then it shouldn't be too hard to reassure them. Secondly, if there is something for them to get jealous about then you should apologize for not handling the situation differently.

For example, here's a situation that happens quite commonly in relationships. A boy will flirt with your girlfriend. Your girlfriend, out of concern for that boys feelings and out of discretion for not wanting to appear rude will normally let the occasion slide. Thus, you would find out about this situation and get upset. Your girlfriend however was only trying to do the right thing. Now would be a good time to talk things out with her. Maybe have a conversation that looks something like, "It upsets me when I find out that boys are flirting with you, I understand that you probably aren't telling them that it's inappropriate to flirt with you because you don't want to make an awkward situation or hurt anyone's feelings or you don't want to be rude when someone is only joking around. I also understand that because our relationship is so strong, you figure that there are less consequences when you hurt me a little compared to a friendly relationship with someone you hardly know that might not be able to hold up to the criticism. But I think that because I'm so important to you and because you love me, I should be a priority when it comes down to who is going to get their feelings hurt. If I haven't done anything wrong but I'm still the one that gets his feelings hurt even though the other boy is doing something wrong than it is a little unfair that I should come second.

Now of course the above situation goes over a lot easier if you aren't letting the same things happen. Now, you're other train of thought might be "Why the heck should anyone care about flirting?" That's a very big question to approach and the "Checking Out Girls and Flirting" chapter approaches it in more detail, however it should be noted that flirting is a bad thing because it is only something that should be shared between two people and it sends out a message other than what's intended. Girls and boys can easily be "led on" by flirting, since flirting was primarily developed as a way to say "I'm interested in you." Even if both parties know it doesn't mean anything serious, it's still used for that purpose and so eventually something is bound to be misinterpreted, also it's a risky game to play.

Here are some other verses from the bible about jealousy and love. Song of Songs 8:6 says, "Place me like a seal over your heart, like a seal on your arm; for love is as strong as death, its jealousy unyielding as the grave. It burns like blazing fire, like a mighty flame. The beginning of Song of Songs 2:16 says, "My lover is mine and I am his;" This verse expresses a clear sense of mutual possession. There is nothing wrong with wanting the one you love to be completely yours as long as you too want to be completely theirs.

Proverbs 6:30-36 expresses how deeply jealousy is rooted into a man's heart and warns against agitating this jealousy but doesn't warn against having the jealousy in the first place. "Men do not despise a thief if he steals to satisfy his hunger when he is starving. Yet if he is caught, he must pay sevenfold, though it costs him all the wealth of his house. But a man who commits adultery lacks judgment; whoever does so destroys himself. Blows and disgrace are his lot, and his shame will never be wiped away; for jealousy arouses a husband's fury, and he will show no mercy when he takes revenge. He will not accept any compensation; he will refuse the bribe, however great it is."

Submission

Submission. A taboo word.

"To yield to or to comply with the will of another." A taboo definition.

"Wives should be submissive to their husbands." A taboo sentence.

Ephesians 5:22 "Wives, submit to your husbands as to the Lord." A taboo verse.

Why?

Why doesn't society like this term? What's so taboo about it? Is there even anything wrong with it? Well maybe. There could be something wrong with it. But there is anything inherently wrong with it. Like food. Food is good. It's great. But it doesn't have to be. It could be poisoned, or you could simply eat too much food. Then that food would be bad for you. So what's my point? Pure submission, the way it was supposed to be, is a good thing. I think we need to give submission another chance.

I have many feministic friends who hear "submission" and get very defensive. As if it's an offensive hurtful term. It's a sad state we live in, when something like "submission" can be twisted and manipulated so much that it makes girls fear the very concept.

But once again, it isn't their fault. It's our fault; Men who have abused the term "submission." So perhaps they don't understand the full concept. Perhaps it would help to untwist it. Submission describes the attitude of someone in relation to someone else. In other words, submission is only possible when two people have a relationship. So when, in a relationship is it good to submit?

It's good to submit when you are in a loving relationship. What are real genuine loving relationships about? Whenever you ask an older couple who's been successfully married for fifty plus years they all tell you the same thing. They're about sacrifice. Sometimes sacrifice is a really great thing. Sometimes it's easier to sacrifice material things instead of sacrificing one's own will or one's own desires.

But sacrificing things that are worth more to you is certainly more meaningful than sacrificing things you don't really care about. And sacrificing your will or desire for your boyfriend's happiness may be a great sacrifice. Anyone who can do that is a person who can love.

Love is about sacrifice. And submission is the greatest kind of sacrifice. So by default, submission is one of the greatest ways to show your love. In concept, it isn't anything to be afraid of or get defensive about. You can forget presents, and dates and romance and sex, but submission, that's where the beauty is at. Submission is the best way to show someone love. Think about the message the gospels tell. Even if you aren't Christian just picture this scene unfold in your mind. Even if you don't think its real, try and just find the beauty in it and imagine how great your relationship could be if you followed this example.

God, completely holy, completely powerful, infinitely better than us, hears the cries of his creation. He looks down, he sees people sinning, people living unhappily, people being abused and mistreated, people who have lost their way, people who are worshipping things that aren't real, and don't give them satisfaction. So what does he do? Does he get angry at our betrayal? No, He sends his son down to Earth. He takes Jesus, who has been in heaven and is infinitely royal and holy, and he sends him down to live with humans, and he gives him a human form to live in, and he's forced to live like a human. Jesus, Son of God, used to being worshipped by heavenly creatures takes the form and life of a mere human being. And then God tells Jesus that he has to die for us, the ultimate submission. God submits to us, because he loves us! Jesus submitted to God because he loves us, and he loves God. If God isn't afraid of submission than why are you? It's beautiful! Submission is amazing! I hope you understand. Look, God will submit to humans, but you're too good to do it? Why?

There's probably a very good reason. As a matter of fact I think there are several good reasons. First of all, I think one factor that contributes to women being unwilling to submit to a man is pride. I think that sometimes people are way too prideful to be willing to change what they want or to lay down what they want, for someone else.

But I don't think that's the only reason. I don't think we can just blame women and be done with it.

I think a much larger portion of the blame should be attributed to men. People submit to God all the time. Women submit to God all the time. Men submit to God all the time. No one thinks to themselves that they are too good to submit to God. Why is this? God is worthy of our submission. But men, most men have absolutely no right to ask a woman to submit to them. God is worthy of our submission because he is righteous. The only apparent way that men could ever expect their women to submit to them is if they were righteous and deserving of submission, which most men aren't. Once a man is worthy of a woman's submission, she would see no problem in submitting to him, because if she is a righteous woman, than most of the time their will would be aligned. And when it wasn't, she could know to trust him to make the right decision. They could even have a discussion on the problem and work it out together. What a world that would be!

But of course, it's pretty ridiculous to assume that a human could ever be as righteous as God. So how can a man justify asking a woman to submit? Well, from a biblical standpoint, God has told women to submit to their husbands (and if this upsets you, don't give up... There's more on the topic a bit further down.) And because God has told women to submit to their husbands, than they should. They should do it for their own sake and for God's sake. You see, if a woman doesn't want to submit to their husband but does so anyway out of obedience to God, than they are really submitting to God. Now, it should be noted that women shouldn't always submit to their husbands. If their husband wants them to do something that is against God's will, then you would do them more honor by not listening to them.

We can't just blame women for not being willing to submit. Especially if men are well known for being prejudice against them and thinking that they are worth less then men, especially if men abuse and take advantage of women.

So let's talk about the bible verse mentioned earlier. Ephesians 5:22. But let's tack on a couple more sentences so we can see the verse as it's originally meant to be used. So we can see the whole context of it. Ephesians 5:22-24: Wives, submit to your husbands as to the Lord. For the husband is the head of the wife as Christ is the head of the church, his body, of which he is the Savior. Now as the church submits to Christ, so also wives should submit to their husbands in everything.

This verse alone, states that wives should submit to their husbands as they also submit to the Lord. In other words, love your husbands like you love Christ and submit to their will as quickly as you would submit to the Lord's will. And it also justifies why, explaining that the wife is like the church of God and the husband is like Christ (relationally), and says that wives should follow their husband, just as the church would follow Jesus. Now some of you reading this are probably skeptical and you probably think this sounds unfair and sexist. But there are verses that follow shed even more light.

Ephesians 25-33 tells husbands how they are supposed to treat their wives: Husbands, love your wives, just as Christ loved the church and gave himself up for her to make her holy, cleansing her by the washing with water through the word, and to present her to himself as a radiant church, without stain or wrinkle or any other blemish, but holy and blameless. In this same way, husbands ought to love their wives as their own bodies. He who loves his wife loves himself. After all, no one ever hated his own body, but he feeds and cares for it, just as Christ does the church—for we are members of his body. 31"For this reason a man will leave his father and mother and be united to his wife, and the two will become one flesh." This is a profound mystery—but I am talking about Christ and the church. However, each one of you also must love his wife as he loves himself, and the wife must respect her husband.

Let's go through this verse by verse. It doesn't tell husbands to submit to their wives. But it tells them to love their wives. Which would mean that they aught to submit to their wives. But even if the husbands weren't positive that that's what "love your wives" meant, they would keep reading and it would say "love your wives just as Christ loved the church and gave himself up for her." In other words, love your wife so much that you would die for her, as Christ died for the church. And how was the church treating Christ when he died? Not too well, they were denying him, mocking him, trading him in for silver and killing him. The church was betraying him, but Christ still died for the church, and that's the kind of love that God commands men to have for their women, to be so submissive that even when their wives are betraying them, they would continue to do anything they could to help their wife. This means that men should be willing to die for their wives and women should be willing to live for their husbands.

Then it talks about the unique connection between man and wife that manifests as a result of sex. This will be touched on, in the Sex chapter. It talks about how man should protect and nurture his wife. It compares the relationship of husband and wife as husband being the head, and the wife being the body. It shows that without each other the two could not exist. And it talks about how you should love your wife and take care of her, just as you nurture your own body with food and treat it like a temple of God, you should also love your wife and care for her in the same way. You need to take care of each other and love each other and equally submit to each other. Submission is not such a bad thing, in reality, it is Godly, loving, generous, and even strong (because trust me, for most women it takes a lot of strength to have to submit, and for most men it takes even more strength to submit.)

Now, I'd also like to talk about a profound and yet simple concept that my brother recently brought to my attention which he learned from marriage counseling at his church.

Men and women are inherently different. And so we experience love in different ways. Women experience love through adoration and what most people would consider to be love actions. Men however, experience love in an entirely different way. Men experience love through respect. Now, in the verse analyzed above God calls men to love their wives but tells women to submit to their husbands. Why not just say that husband and wives should love each other? Why must the women submit? Well, the truth is that God is telling each person what they need to hear. Wives aren't called to love their husbands because that comes naturally. Women are naturally filled with evident selfless love. What they aren't filled with is eagerness to submit. On the other hand, men are not filled with this desire to love and more often than not they end up forgetting how much their wife needs affection and attention and love, and God wants them to remember. So he reminds them each individually of things they both need to work on.

But how the verse summarizes itself may be the most important issue. Ephesians 5:33 "33However, each one of you also must love his wife as he loves himself, and the wife must respect her husband." The word respect has replaced the word submission. Because if you respect your husband enough, you would submit to them, just as when you respect God enough you submit to him. This is very important, because this is how men experience love, through respect, and ultimately, through submission.

Now you can see even this concept has outlasted the ravages of time and culture. When men make business deals, they demand respect, when the drug dealer on the street works with his pushers and fiends, he demands respect, and when a father talks to his son he demands respect. Men love respect and each man knows that inherently they deserve to be respected. But women don't know this about man because women aren't men and how could they be expected to know especially when our culture tells them otherwise? The truth is, if you want to show love to a man, you must respect him.

Which brings us to our next point, if women should submit to their husbands, and husbands should submit to their wives, what happens when both disagree? Who gets the say in the end of it? The husband does. Because you married him, which means he's worthy of your love, which means he is worthy of your respect. Inherently worthy of your respect because he is your husband and you should live for him, just as he should live for you. Now it seems unfair, but listen, men need to love their wives no matter what; at the end of the day God commands them to love their wives. Because that's how women experience love and find happiness and fulfillment in their marriage. But women need to submit to their husbands no matter what because at the end of the day God commands a woman to submit and respect her husband because that's how he finds happiness and fulfillment in his marriage.

UNDERSTANDING

It is important to understand each other in a relationship in order to love. We must constantly put ourselves in each others place. Often times, many arguments come up as simple misunderstandings. It is important to talk to one another and discuss our thoughts and feelings. Many people know this and in the heat of an argument they forget this. We must be patient with one another.

It is important to recognize, first and foremost that no one will ever be perfect. When I said love demands forgiveness, this is what I was referring to. Many people will make mistakes. Many people will do things they shouldn't do. We all have things we regret. We've heard it been said "regret nothing, life is too short." Well, I urge you to regret. It is better to do things that we *don't have to regret*, because the truth is, life *is* too short. But just in case you aren't perfect and you end up doing something you should regret, it is important to regret. Regret ensures that you will not make the same mistake twice. Regret shows that you are sorry and it shows that you recognize making a mistake. It is healthy to regret. Do not obsess on the past. Live in the present, live for the future, but a small amount of regret is healthy and vital for the progression of a relationship.

If you make a mistake in your relationship, do not hide it. Confront your mistake. If you let it brood in you, if you keep quiet, thinking that your partner is better off not knowing, you are demeaning the value of your relationship. You are sacrificing a part of your relationship. You will always feel bad about this mistake, you will always think that you do not deserve your partner and it will come out in your actions. From this point on you will always think that you are a bad boyfriend and so you will start behaving like a bad boyfriend.

You must show that you are sorry, you must ask for forgiveness. Perhaps forgiveness will not be given to you, hopefully, if you are truly sorry than it will be given to you, but there is always a chance. You may say to yourself, "I'd rather hold this in and keep my girlfriend than lose her." The truth is, you will be living a lie. You won't really have her; someone who she thinks you are will have her. She will love the man that you aren't. Not to mention, if you do love her, you would recognize that she has a right to know.

Please, I beg you to confess your mistakes, whether it is infidelity, or a lie, or anything else, you must take it head on. If your relationship doesn't collapse under the pressure, it will grow stronger. It may feel like it has taken a step backward but the truth is, you were already back there when you kept the secret from your partner, now you are progressing to a stronger truer relationship. You want your relationship to be invulnerable, impenetrable. You want to have a love so strong that you can laugh at anything that makes an attempt to come between you. This is the only way to achieve it. The problem will never leave on its own.

If your partner comes to you asking for forgiveness; if she has done something you never thought she would do, you must forgive her. If you love her more than anything in the world and if she truly feels sorry, you must find it in you heart to forgive her. In the end, losing her completely will be a grave mistake. If you love her, than she would not be so easy to let go so quickly. You must remember this, no matter how hurt you are. If she truly regrets what she has done, she will never do it again. This is what you've always wanted. Recognize that she isn't perfect. Recognize that she has made a mistake. Do everything in your power to keep her. Do everything in your power to see past this moment. Seek counseling if you have to, whatever it takes. Surely, if you love her, this will not be such a great sacrifice. Love has the strength to overcome a mistake, no matter how deep it may hurt you. Your trust may feel like it has been destroyed. Time heals all wounds and you will learn to trust again. Now you at least have further assurance that it will not happen again. If she truly regrets what she has done, it will not happen again.

If you have been betrayed by your partner, if she has made a mistake, if she has cheated on you, if she has given into temptation, recognize that she is not perfect. When it comes time for you to make a mistake, you will be able to confidently ask for forgiveness. Confessing her mistake is a sign of trust. Confessing her mistake is a sign of love. Do not take such a thing for granted, it is a blessing. Many would be deceitful and continue to lie, if she truly feels bad, break down your pride and forgive her. You are not too good for her. You never were, not if you loved her. Love demands forgiveness, be wise, and do not be prideful and arrogant. Do not hold a grudge, a man who holds a grudge is worth as much as that man who has hurt him, because it is wrong to not forgive and so if you hold a grudge, you have become just as bad as the one who wronged you.

I should make a point very clear before I begin any further. It is important to have love for yourself, before you worry about having love for anyone else. Therefore, if you are in an abusive relationship you must take this matter seriously. Love yourself and respect yourself enough to get out of this unhealthy relationship. Do not feel that because you love him...or who he used to be...that you should automatically let him back into your life. Love is something both partners need to nurture and help grow. One cannot do it all on his or her own.

Men and women are different. Men and women think differently. Try to think like her in situations where you cannot find understanding. Try to see what she sees. You do not like soap operas and she does not find interest in hunting deer. We were built differently and quite naturally, we think differently on many subjects. When you were pulling the legs off of spiders she was out playing hopscotch. You may be republican while she may be democratic. Love does not discriminate. Do not let political views come between your love. Realize that you both think differently and you both have different priorities. She may be more apt to wanting to help others while you may be more concerned with self preservation. Do not take this for granted either. It is good to be balanced. Allow her to be your other half. Take her views seriously. This may involve compromise, this may involve sacrifice. Love demands sacrifice. Love every part of your partner. I guarantee you, if you love your partner and lose her; you will miss every part of her, even the parts that you thought you couldn't stand. Why? Because, that is what makes her who she is. The way she chews with her mouth open, the way she speaks her mind on a sensitive subject with people she does not know. If those are things about your girlfriend that you can't stand, then remember that is part of the girl that you loved and you will find yourself missing the girl that you loved, if you let something come between you.

"Allow her to be your other half." I want to focus on this statement for a second. God created man and woman in his image. However you and I can tell that men and women are uniquely different. A popular theory on this is that man is one part of God and woman is another part of God. I believe this to be evidently true. I believe that sometimes God is soft and gentle like a woman's touch while other times he can be angry and violent with the passion of a man. I believe that the reason sex is a merging of flesh is because our souls strive to be like God and strive to be whole, and the way for a man to be whole is to be one person with the woman he loves.

Many times men get caught up in trying to be a provider. We always hear about "the woman behind the man." Do not allow this to happen. Allow her to be a part of your life. Do not push her into the background. Walk together. Allow her to be the woman beside the man. Make decisions together. Be a team. Do not seize control of every situation. Do not make her decisions for her. Allow her to play a vital role in your life. She will soon grow tired of just existing. She will want to live, just like you will want to live. She will want to take risks, she will want adventure, she will want drama, she will want action, and she will not want to grow stale.

In the Garden of Eden, Adam was given important work, this is because God knew Adam would become bored of things if God was taking care of Adam's whole life and gave him nothing to do, so God gave him fulfilling work to do, like naming the animals. I don't really know of any other work, mostly because I wasn't there, but I'm sure God could've thought of something. The point is, God could've easily named the animals but he wanted Adam to feel fulfilled and proud and have a life with meaning. Therefore do not get caught up in "taking care" of your wife (or you know, girlfriend). She is not an infant. She is quite independent. Do not allow yourselves to take over every aspect of her life. Love her and share things with her.

There is nothing wrong with being a provider for your wife; if you do not want your wife to work, then good for you. But she may want to. And if she does not want to, you must still share her in the decision making process when you spend money. It is not your money, it is both of yours. If she thinks something is too expensive, then you must make a compromise and perhaps change your mind about buying it. You are a team. You must work together in all aspects of life. If you want to take care of your girlfriend, involve her in life, not just money but all aspects of your life.

It is important to function as a team and work things out together. It is good to strengthen the bond between you by creating an environment of cooperation and co-dependency. If you want to become close to your wife then it is important to work as one person. Now obviously, this can't be all the time. I'm not suggesting that a husband should have to go to his wife's basket weaving class if he doesn't want to. And I'm not suggesting that a wife should have to go to the super bowl with her husband if she'd rather not be embarrassed by his loud screaming and grunting. Obviously it is just as good to have alone time and be able to take some time off and just be by yourself but it is good to make sure your wife is a part of your life and that she plays a crucial role in your decision making process.

TRUST

Another important aspect in a relationship is trust. If trust isn't there, your relationship can't function properly. If trust isn't there, then love cannot thrive.

One easy way to gain trust in a relationship is to let your partner know that you are not driven by sexual desires or "needs". It is not uncommon for the boyfriend in a relationship to want sexual pleasures. It is not uncommon for boys to say they "need sexual pleasures". What I mean is sometimes a boy will say "If we don't mess around sometime soon, I will go insane." And then of course the girl can take this as a compliment that the boy needs her in order to be happy in life. And it is seemingly innocent and a fun way to joke around and let your partner know that you miss her, or whatever.

But it does have degenerative effects on a relationship, especially the trust aspect of a relationship.

For example, my girlfriend and I are in a long distance relationship. We live six and a half hours away from each other (by car) and a lot of time goes by when she isn't with me. So I felt it was necessary that she knew I didn't need to fulfill my sexual desires. I made it a point to tell her, that we don't need to do anything sexually until marriage. I wanted her to know that I could have self control.

If I didn't do this, if I had pretended to need sexual pleasure from her than it wouldn't be unreasonable for her to get scared that I would still need sexual pleasure while we weren't together. It would be understandable if there was a lack of trust. But now that she knows I have self control and don't need physical pleasure when we're together, she can trust that I don't need it when we aren't together, which is, most of the time. And It's more important to have trust in a relationship, than it is to have sexual pleasure, If you don't see it this way, just keep reading.

But now even if we did live next door from each other and I did see her all the time I would still feel it was just as important to practice self control and let her know I didn't need anything physical from her because there would be times when I would go away. Let's say, I took a three week vacation from her. For our entire relationship I would be joking around about how I needed her to satisfy my cravings for her and all of the sudden, I would leave for three weeks and I would expect her to think that now, for no reason at all, I stopped needing sexual pleasure? I would expect her to think that just because we are apart, I'm no longer the same man? No, that would be absurd. And so she would be justified to think that I might cheat on her, because all this time I've been a man without self control, because all this time, I've needed to give into my sexual desires. And so this three week vacation of mine could possibly be absolute hell for her.

And could I get upset with her for not trusting me? No, I'm the one who has been fortifying it in her mind the entire time that I needed to have sexual satisfaction in order to function properly throughout my life.

If you want to have a trusting relationship and if you want to get rid of jealousy and insecurity, than let your girlfriend know that you have self control. And practice it when you are not only apart but also when you are together, so that the two of you can have the strongest relationship possible. So that nothing could come in your way. That's what this book is all about; creating an everlasting relationship.

Children and Parents

I mentioned children earlier. I love children, and this chapter is for teenagers as much as it is for adults because it is a good viewpoint for all to see.

I believe I would do anything for my children, many people in college or high school will get an abortion because they aren't ready for a kid or don't have time for one. (This is also a good reason for waiting until marriage, that way you will be ready to have a kid and if it happens accidentally you will be just as happy, after all having a kid should be a thing to celebrate and embrace). I would die for my children, so how is it that I wouldn't be able to stop going to school for them? How could I not be willing to change my whole life for my children? The point is, when it comes time to have children, we should love and embrace them. They should be the best part of your life and your number one priority. You should be able to make any sacrifice for them to make their lives better and more fulfilling.

Now, this won't be an anti-abortion rant because that is not what this book is about and it is not why you are reading it. What I want to discuss is how we should treat children and how sons and daughters should expect to be treated.

I have no children of my own and at one point I thought that I should not add this chapter because I do not have much experience with having children. But then my father corrected me and reminded me that I was once a child and therefore have every right to speak about how children should be treated and what they should be taught.

As I mentioned in my introduction, there are many things that I regret in my life and many things that I wish I would've known sooner. One of the best ways for me to have gotten the knowledge and wisdom that I wish I had when I was younger would be through my parents. Sometimes I think, had my parents talked to me and explained to me the value of sexual discrepancy and told me how I should treat women and why, I would've been able to make better choices, not only for me but for other people.

I regret most of my behavior during my first relationship. It started in ninth grade and went till about the end of the tenth grade (if I recall correctly, which I usually don't). I wasn't a very good boyfriend. I liked this girl that I was dating but I certainly failed at showing it sometimes. I was a big flirt, and constantly flirted with other girls, including her friends, and not only when I was away from her but even in front of her. She didn't seem to mind most of the time and when she did express concern I would justify myself by saying, "it's just harmless fun." Well, I later found out that it wasn't harmless fun. Not only due to what I explained earlier but it most likely played a big role in the downfall of our relationship which completely destroyed me for a good couple of months. We dated for about a year and a half, and believe it or not, at the time, I wouldn't have had any problem with marrying her. I was head over heels for this girl, she was the first girl I ever dated seriously, and she was also my first kiss. And while I'm now glad that it did end so that I could date the girl I have now and fall in love with her. I wish things would've ended differently.

You see, after our relationship ended she moved onto even worse relationships and I, in part, feel guilty about that because I had the chance to show her how she deserved to be treated and show her that she could demand respect and that she deserved to be treated better. Instead she probably subconsciously assumed that I was as good as it gets and therefore she didn't think she should expect anything better from anyone else. That is a huge danger of being a bad boyfriend.

I'm proud these days to be such a decent boyfriend for the girl that I'm dating now. I'm ecstatic that she gets to be treated the way she deserves to be. She has so far gotten the best of me. And to be honest, I thank God for showing me the way to becoming a good boyfriend and I do think that Christian teachings and my Christian mentors have played a vital role in showing me how to be a good boyfriend.

As parents, we have the responsibility to pass on what we've learned in life and to raise our children with strong values and morals so they can enter in strong loving relationships and can live without regrets.

It might be a very awkward thing to do. Talking to your children about porn and sex and dating is never an easy topic. But to be honest, it gets easier as it goes. And it opens new doors for trust and communication. If your child can feel comfortable talking to you about sex and porn then he can come to you when he has questions of his own about drugs or sex or his body. Not only does it open those doors but the bond between parent and child will strengthen from it. So I think the awkwardness would be an easy enough sacrifice for all the good things that would come of it. Besides, how selfish would it be if you did not talk to your own child because of a little potential awkwardness?

Now, here's a bad piece of advice for you to tell your children. "Minimize potential hurt." I've been told this before and I've heard other people repeat it in different ways. "Too young to be so serious," is another one. Now here's my take on this. When people say "minimize potential hurt," what they're really saying is to not invest too many feelings and too much time. That way, when the "inevitable" break-up comes, no one will cry, no one will be heart broken, and no one will care at all. Now I would pose the question: then why date at all? Why date if you won't give it your all? Why date for such temporary reasons? Why date with the assumption that it will end. If you don't give it your all, how will you ever know if the relationship is going to be fulfilling or not? Why date without the intention of loving? It would be more of a physical relationship then anything else, more of a waste of time than anything else. The heartbreak is worth the memories made and the love that's been shared. Now don't get me wrong and think that by me saying "give it your all" I mean that you should start having sex and what not, I would assume that by after you read this you would think that when I said "give it your all" that would include waiting till marriage to have sex, because that is a bigger sign of love than having sex before marriage. So be sure to check out the sex chapter before you set this book down for the last time.

Another piece of advice that I was never a big fan of is telling children "you should date around and make sure a guy is perfect for you." That's ridiculous. If you've got someone that makes you wonderfully happy, why do you need to date someone else in order for you to reestablish what you already know? It's hard to understand why people wouldn't be happy if they just dated one person their entire life. It's hard to understand why so many people think their children are "too young to be with just one person." As if, being with multiple unfulfilling purely physical relationships would be somehow healthier. It's upsetting to say the least and not only that but it doesn't make much sense at all.

I've also noticed that it's been a common trend lately for some parents to actually encourage their children to have sex. I have several friends whose parents have gone as far as telling their children that they want to get them birth control. Now, I'm not against birth control if someone is having sex, but what I am against is telling your child they need to get on birth control so that when they start having sex they will be prepared. That's pretty much like saying "Hey, it's normal for you to be having sex soon." How is this child supposed to feel? Well if they haven't had sex yet and their parents are assuming they are having sex than they might feel a little pressured to have sex, and they certainly wouldn't have the slightest idea that there may be something wrong with having sex since their parents are taking such a casual position on the whole thing. It's ridiculous, at least give your child somewhat of a chance.

I talked to one my ex-girlfriends parents once. I asked them whether or not they regretted having sex with people other than each other. They said no.

It wasn't much of a surprise and I guess it's because of the way the world functions. You see, there are three reasons why people encourage their children to have sex before marriage.

The first and most obvious reason is because they don't know any better or don't agree with the morals and values discussed earlier.

The second reason that parents would encourage their children to have sex is the bandwagon effect. People like it when they aren't alone. We want people to be in the same boat as us. If you were to get high, you would want your friends to get high with you. So sometimes parents will want their children to do the same things they did. You don't want to feel alone because if you were the only one doing it then you might realize you were wrong.

This brings us right into the third reason for encouraging your children to have sex before marriage. You see, if you were to actually tell your children to wait until marriage, then you would pretty much be admitting that you made the wrong choice. And not too many people are willing to do this; sometimes this is because of pride. Sometimes it's because: if you admit that you are wrong, than you have to face the guilt, and let's be honest...no one really wants to feel guilty.

So because of this cowardice, parents will drag their children down with them and will encourage them to ruin their chance of having the most fulfilling life possible.

Part II

Responsibilities and Behaviors of a Boyfriend

We all have temptations. We should consider it a blessing to have temptations. Temptations are not to be given in to. We have temptations so that we are able to show our love through obedience. In the bible, the book of James Chapter 1 verse 2 says: "Consider it pure joy, my brothers, whenever you face trials of many kinds, because you know that the testing of your faith develops perseverance."

Everyone is tempted and there is no way to eliminate temptation. However there are ways to *limit* temptation. For example, if one is tempted to watch pornography, then to limit this temptation he must get rid of his internet connection or stop buying magazines. There is however, no excuse to giving into a tempting situation. It's simply weakness; weakness in morals, in character, in the ability to consider consequences of actions. There isn't any good excuse. The only excuse is personal weakness.

In the following chapters we'll address those temptations, mostly ones that directly affect a relationship. We'll discuss flirting with other girls, checking other girls out, talking to friends on the phone at one in the morning, hanging out with friends of the opposite sex in a one on one environment, watching pornography, masturbation, cheating on your girlfriend, lying to your girlfriend, sexual activities with your girlfriend, sex, and maybe some other things.

The statements will be reinforced using logic and reasoning. Also use scripture from the bible will be used and a lot of first hand experiences or stories that and hypothetical situations to make things as clear as possible.

Learning what to do and not what to do is great but if you don't know why things are wrong or right then you won't be able to behave the right way for very long.

"Checking Out" Girls and Flirting

I used to be a pro at flirting and checking girls out. I was a born natural at it. I suppose parts of me thought it was wrong. However, my general understanding of it was that it was harmless, and I was always able to justify it somehow or another when my previous girlfriends had expressed concerns. Little did I know that my behavior would lead to inevitably unhealthy relationships and not only break-ups but also the girlfriends that I had treated badly would never expect or insist to be treated better by their future boyfriends.

First, we'll address: checking girls out. It is irresponsible to allow ones' self to give into temptations. If we see a beautiful girl, we should leave it at that. We should not stare. We should not look back. We can justify staring and looking back by saying "it is a beautiful creation", "it is like looking at a sunrise", and "we are admiring God's work." These are lies. A sunrise cannot flirt. We cannot talk to a sunrise nor have a relationship with a sunrise. We do not look at a sunrise the way we look at a girl. If that were the case, you should not look at a sunrise either. We find women beautiful because they have a certain amount of sex appeal. We enjoy looking at them because of the feelings and emotions it invokes. However you should make it an effort to only get pleasure from looking at your girlfriend. You should keep things sacred between you.

I have a relative who allows her husband to gawk at other women. She says "I know its harmless fun, its not like he would ever approach them, so I let him." This "harmless fun" theory couldn't be farther from the truth. I know I'm guilty of using it as an excuse too. I know that it's very common for people to say this.

However, it isn't harmless fun because it is harming your relationship. By looking at that girl you may be comparing her to your girlfriend and subconsciously you may be setting unrealistic expectations for her, thus decreasing your attraction to your girlfriend and the value or appreciation that you have for her. If you love your girlfriend then the last thing you want to do is purposefully lower the amount in which you appreciate her. It is selfish of you to behave in such a way that you are willing to hinder your love in exchange for giving into temptations and enjoying the looks of a complete stranger.

Not only is it bad for your girlfriend but perhaps it is bad for the girl you are looking at. For example, maybe you're looking at her because of the skimpy clothes she is wearing. You're telling her that the more she dresses like that, the more attention she will get. Instead of showing her that she is someone who has dignity and that she deserves to be treated like a person. In addition, you do not know this woman and you do not have an intimate relationship with her so you have absolutely no right to get pleasure from her body.

If you are a Christian then you have to recognize that God is king. This means that we are his children, and even more than that it means that we are his princes and princesses. This is no way to treat a princess. This is no way to treat God's child. A woman's beauty and our attraction to them is most certainly a gift from God. It is no accident that we are so physically attracted to women. However, this attraction is reserved for people in loving relationships. We are abusing our freedom and our gift of attraction if we allow ourselves to get pleasure from women outside of a relationship with them.

I would take it a step further and say that people are temples for the Holy Spirit and should be treated with love and respect, the same kind of love and respect that you would want to treat God with. The writers of the New Testament and God himself would urge you to treat others the way you would treat Jesus Christ. Think about that.

The bible is very clear on lust. Lust, as defined by the American heritage dictionary is "intense or unrestrained sexual craving." Certainly, lust can be very relative to checking girls out. Our attraction to girls comes from hormones, it comes from a sexual attraction. In other words, we are feeding our sexual cravings when we check girls out. We are giving into lust.

One of the commandments is thou shall not covet. In other words, we shouldn't want what someone else has. The girl you are checking out is not yours. She does not belong to you; therefore you are coveting what isn't yours. And perhaps she isn't in a relationship now but you can bet she will be one day, and she could even get married one day. And therefore you are coveting someone's wife. This is clearly wrong and God has directly said so.

To exemplify this, the Bible provides us with a book, the book of Job. Job was a very righteous man; a man of God. The book starts out with Satan wanting to test humans, and God tells Satan to test Job, because Job was the most righteous human and God had faith that he could pass Satan's test. Since Job was such a favored man of God, Christians should take what he has to say very seriously. Job says in Job 31:9-12[1]:

9 "If my heart has been enticed by a woman, or if I have lurked at my neighbor's door, 10 then may my wife grind another man's grain, and may other men sleep with her. 11 For that would have been shameful, a sin to be judged. 12 It is a fire that burns to Destruction; it would have uprooted my harvest."

Job admits that even if he just thought about a woman, if he felt an urge to approach a woman, and if he felt compelled to approach her or if he even gave it serious thought then he was at fault. That he was guilty. And he admits that a justified punishment for this would be for his wife to leave him. This is how serious God considers checking out other girls, and lusting after them is.

God is very clear on how his children should be treated and as followers of God we are expected to follow his will, and not only that but we are expected to follow his will due to the fact that God only gives us rules for our own benefit. He shows us the way to have fullness in life. He wants us to be happy. Like when a parent tells his child not to stray too far from home when they go outside. It is for the good of the child. It is out of love that they do this, and it is out of Gods love that he gives us direction in life.

Now when I was confronted with this by my Young Life leader (which I mentioned in the introduction) while I was in high school, I said to him "but I don't think about having sex with these women that I check out, and even if I were to imagine having sex with them, its not like I would take it seriously, because I'm waiting till marriage so its pure fiction and fantasy." The truth is it doesn't really matter at all whether you seriously think about having sex with the girls that you are checking out or not. You are still giving into sexual desires, sexual cravings. You still get sexual pleasure from it. And it still has the same consequences. You still set unrealistic standards for your girlfriend. Whether you have a girlfriend or not, you are making it so that what you become attracted to becomes more and more defined and raises the bar. For instance, if you check out

Victoria Secret models all the time, then you are less likely to be attracted to the girl down the street as much as you would've been if you weren't looking at Victoria Secret models. And you might say, well I'm smart enough to realize that the girl I love isn't going to look perfect. But the truth is, it doesn't matter how smart and practical you are, you will still appreciate her beauty less. It's a very selfish thing to do.

To simplify and recap all that was discussed: By checking girls out you may be comparing her to your girlfriend and subconsciously you may be setting unrealistic expectations for her, thus decreasing your attraction to your girlfriend and the value or appreciation that you have for your girlfriend. If you love your girlfriend then the last thing you want to do is purposefully lower the amount in which you appreciate her.

I'd like to make one thing straight though. If you see a beautiful girl, you have done nothing wrong. God did create her. And he did create her to be beautiful and to be attractive to men. It is natural to see a beautiful girl, it is not a sin. However it becomes a sin when you seek to get those attraction pleasures from people other then your girlfriend. And perhaps you don't have a girlfriend, it is still wrong to "check out" beautiful women and gawk at them and stare because you are treating her as an object. Women have dignity and should be respected and treated as people, not sunsets, not works of art, not sex objects, but people. I will admit that you can admire a girl's beauty, and it wouldn't be wrong. For example, if you had a daughter and thought she was beautiful, obviously, it isn't because of sexual attraction. You love your daughter and appreciate her life. You can see an interesting girl, and look at her, and perhaps you are looking because she has a unique face or something that is uncommon and so you aren't looking out of sexual attraction but rather, mere interest. I would caution you however and tell you not to try and justify staring at girls and to keep yourself in check to be sure that you are living a righteous life.

Here's a realistic situation which I've heard a number of times in different situations to reinforce what I am saying. I'm sitting at the beach with my girlfriend and two beautiful girls walk right in front of us, wearing extremely flattering bikinis. I have several options.

Option number one is, I can stare and treat these women like objects and degrade them. I can stare and make my girlfriend feel jealous and hurt. I can stare and raise my expectations for what most girls should look like (including my girlfriend). I can stare and compare their bodies to that of my girlfriends (even subconsciously) and thus lower the appreciation I have for my girlfriend. All this I could do. And it is all bad. And when people think they are "appreciating a person's beauty like a fine piece of art" and thinking that it doesn't have bad effects, they are lying to themselves and others.

Option two is, I could turn to my girlfriend and say "those are the ugliest two women I have ever seen." Which is a direct lie, and not only that but your girlfriend will know that you are lying and it will still have degrading affects on your relationship. You should always be honest and truthful in order to establish good trust.

Option three is, you can feel extremely guilty for thinking that those girls are beautiful and ask God to forgive you and think that you would be better off without having eyes.

Or option four, the best and most reasonable option is that you can see those beautiful girls and think to yourself, God is impressive, and sure does know what he's doing when it comes to creating women. And let it go. Don't look back for more.

Don't take it for what it isn't. Don't replay the situation over and over in your mind. And maybe you can even turn to your girlfriend and say. "I love you, you've been with me for a long time, you've struggled with me, you've loved me, you've put up with my crap, you've been a wonderful girlfriend, and there's absolutely no competition here, those girls could never compare to you and could never take your place, and I know that." So ask yourself, which man do you want to be? Which boyfriend do you want to be? Which love are you trying to cultivate?

It is important to point out that there is a lot of wisdom in trying not to see things. I'm not saying you should walk around with your eyes closed and bump into walls, I'm simply saying that if you don't want to be tempted to stare at beautiful women, you shouldn't walk into a beautiful women's convention. In other words: Limit your temptations by the places that you go and the people you surround yourself with. A strip bar is probably not a place for you to walk into if you wish to uphold the morals of a righteous man and a loving boyfriend.

Now onto flirting: as I said, I was a pro at flirting. I would flirt with any girl I could. It didn't matter whether or not I was in the same room with my girlfriend. It didn't matter whether or not I was flirting with my girlfriend's best friends. I pretty much never put boundaries on when or with whom it was appropriate to flirt. This is because I never thought anything was wrong with it.

One of the reasons people have a hard time realizing that certain things are bad for them is because they're fun to do and so they know that if they question it, they might have to stop doing it. So it's easier to not question your actions.

However, the reason that we do question our actions during a relationship is so that we can have better relationships. It is for our own benefit.

Flirting is also giving into temptation. Flirting is something we should save for our partner. Flirting with anyone else is something that would hurt your partner or should hurt your partner. It is foolish to flirt, even when your partner is not around. Do not do something that would hurt your girlfriend if she is present, even when she is not. Flirting is normally done with someone that we like. We may not like them more than our girlfriend and we may not like them enough to date them. So then, why is it worth doing at all if we know it would hurt our partners?

Why does flirting hurt our partners? It's pretty simple. If you flirt with someone, you are indirectly saying "Hey, I'm interested in you." The genius in it is that you aren't actually saying "I'm interested in you" so therefore, it seems like you haven't done anything wrong. But everyone knows that you are misleading girls into thinking that you like them. And you're doing it on purpose. So actually, your girlfriend should be jealous, because you're indirectly telling other girls that you like them. It's foolish and there isn't much to it other than that.

I suppose you could argue, "What if the other girl has a boyfriend, or what if she knows that I don't like her." It doesn't matter. It's still harmful for your girlfriend. And what if your girlfriend doesn't actually care? Well, she should. But regardless, you're giving into temptations. And even if she doesn't care, you should respect her enough to care for her and explain to her why she should care.

Do not hurt the one you love, do not be foolish. Do not give into temptations which would damage your relationship with the one you love. Respect your girlfriends; your love for them is able to overcome any temptation set in your path. Love gives us the strength to do many things, feed your love; do not do something to deteriorate it. These may seem like simple things to say, but it is surprising how many people do not think this way. They let themselves be overcome by temptation and do not second guess whether what they're doing is right or wrong. Perhaps because it feels good, but like all things we must consider the consequences. And while it may feel good to flirt with strangers, it feels even better to be loved by your wife or your girlfriend and to live without guilt; "without regrets."

Cheating

Some words in this chapter seem harsh, and a little demeaning and definitely unsympathetic... If you are turned off by this chapter than please keep reading, the ending is nothing like the beginning. I have only kept the beginning because I believe parts of it have a lot of truth, no matter how crudely it comes across and it's mainly left in order to demonstrate one way of thinking compared to another.

I've got to be honest; I've never cheated on any of my girlfriends. Writing this chapter gets me upset. Upset with people who would take someone for granted. Upset with people who would destroy someone's trust, and self esteem. Upset with someone who would invest so much time and emotion into a relationship only to tear it down.

Why cheat? I've heard tons of excuses. Some excuses aren't as evil as others. I've heard: boredom, drunkenness, being a passionate person, being a spontaneous person, falling in love with the right person at the wrong time, sexual needs, emotional needs, too much time apart, and stupidity. You can bet the list is much longer than that. I have one problem with this list: it's all a load of crap. It's the most cowardice list of excuses I have ever seen. Don't ever cheat on someone you love. Don't ever cheat on someone you are committed to.

It's hard for me to not get frustrated while writing this. Forgive me if I sound judgmental or hateful. I'm passionate about it because I hate seeing people get hurt and totally destroyed.

Let's talk about these excuses. We'll go in order. Boredom; Cheating because you are bored with your current relationship. Why not break up with someone first? Why not talk things out first? How selfish do you have to be to cheat on someone because you are bored of them? If you're guilty of this, then you are quite possibly a bad person. But who am I to say?

Drunkenness; cheating on someone because you are drunk and didn't know any better or because "you just weren't yourself at that time." This is bull. Don't ever believe this. It is a lie. I've heard before, and I think it makes a lot of sense "a drunk mans actions are a sober mans thoughts." In other words, if you are drunk and made out with someone or had sex with someone, it isn't because you are drunk and are a totally different person, it's just because you have carried out the actions of your usual thoughts. You're just as guilty either way. But when you're drunk, you're finally "busted' for being a lustful person. Drunkenness lowers your inhibitions. That's all. It doesn't change your usual desires; it just opens the door more for you to give into them. It isn't a very good excuse at all. And suppose getting drunk did change you into an entirely different person. Then you should be aware of that, and therefore you should think to yourself, maybe I shouldn't get drunk because I'll end up cheating on my girlfriend.

Being passionate and spontaneous; therefore, you are more susceptible to cheating on someone and you just can't help it. If you're using this as an excuse then I'm surprised you would even bother trying to have a relationship. You have put love and commitment on a much lower level. Instead, you would rather seek pleasures and fulfill selfish temporary animalistic desires. It's heartbreaking to hear people use this excuse. It's disgusting.

Falling in love with the right person at the wrong time, in other words, you are in a relationship and sometime during that relationship you have accidentally fallen in love but it was out of your control. You couldn't help it. It was fate, it was destiny, it isn't you're fault. Wrong. Very, very wrong. You can decide not to fall in love with someone. You do have a choice. For example, you wouldn't fall in love with someone who murdered you're family. Why? Because you have the ability to decide who and what you're attracted to. It is only because you have allowed yourself to fall in love with somebody. It is out of personal weakness. Not because you couldn't help it but because you didn't help it, so don't you dare use that as an excuse.

Using sexual needs as an excuse for cheating, in other words, someone wasn't fulfilling your sexual needs so you sought to get fulfillment from someone else. Let's get one thing straight. Sex isn't a need for anything or anyone. Sex isn't necessary for survival (Unless you're talking about the survival of a species... Of course I know we don't even need to have sex in order to reproduce using the technology we have today, so we could probably survive as a species without sex now that I think about it... not that I would ever suggest that.) Sex isn't necessary for functioning as a human being. Sex isn't on the same level as eating or breathing or sleeping. Sex is nothing more than a privilege. You don't need sex, and therefore having sexual needs is a horrible reason for cheating on someone. It is a lie.

Sex is ultimately supposed to be used as an outward expression of love. It's a physical manifestation of the love you have for someone. It's an act of romantic love. So saying that you cheated on the one you love because he wasn't fulfilling your sexual desires is pretty backward reasoning.

Using emotional needs as a reason for cheating on someone is also a lie. In other words, you need to feel appreciated and wanted and loved and sought after. Well, first of all you don't need these things. Secondly, and most importantly, sexual relations should never ever be used for emotional reinforcement. You should never have sex or do sexual things out of lack of self confidence. It is foolish. Again, sex is meant to be an expression of love between two people. It is when you are in love that you should have sex. You shouldn't have sex to get love. Plenty of young girls will give their virginity away for this reason, having sex with boys so that they will love them. They will all tell you this is foolish and that it just doesn't work that way.

Saying that spending too much time apart is why you cheated on someone is also a bad excuse. I'm in a long distance relationship right now. My girlfriend is six and a half hours away. She's all I think about. And sure I get lonely, I miss her, I wish I had her close to me, I wish I could be with someone I love everyday. But guess what. I suck it up. Why? I love her. Nothing could ever make me want to cheat on her. No matter how badly I wanted to feel companionship, I would never hurt her. I would do anything for her so how could I hurt her? How could I voluntarily do something to harm her when I say I'm willing to do anything to make her happy?

Using stupidity for a reason for cheating is a great excuse. It's even forgivable. If you were too dumb to realize that cheating was bad, then sure you could be forgiven. But you should never seek to be in a serious relationship with anyone ever again.

God uses the word adultery when he talks about cheating. Adultery is either when a husband has sex with someone who isn't his wife or when a wife has sex with someone who isn't her husband. However we can clearly connect God's feelings about adultery to God's feelings about people cheating on their girlfriends. If I were to list all the verses in the bible that warn against adultery, no one would want to read them all, so I'll just cover a few, in order to get the point across.

Genesis 20:3 says "But God came to Abimelech in a dream one night and said to him, "You are as good as dead because of the woman you have taken; she is a married woman."" This verse is very similar to Proverbs 6:32 which says "But a man who commits adultery lacks judgment; whoever does so destroys himself."

Exodus 20:14 says very plainly "You shall not commit adultery." And the same verse is repeated in Deuteronomy 5:18 "You shall not commit adultery."

In Jeremiah 7:9-10 it is written, "Will you steal and murder, commit adultery and perjury, burn incense to Baal and follow other gods you have not known, and then come and stand before me in this house, which bears my Name, and say, "We are safe"—safe to do all these detestable things?"

Hosea 4:1-2 says "Hear the word of the Lord, you Israelites, because the Lord has a charge to bring against you who live in the land: "There is no faithfulness, no love, no acknowledgment of God in the land. There is only cursing, lying and murder, stealing and adultery; they break all bounds, and bloodshed follows bloodshed."

So it's pretty obvious that God doesn't want us participating in adultery and infidelity. I've know plenty of people who have been cheated on. I know someone who had a boyfriend that cheated on her on several occasions and even had another girlfriend at the same time. I have no idea how her boyfriend lived with himself or why he thought doing these things was beneficial.

We can see the root of it pretty easily though. It all stems from selfishness. Relationships require you to be as selfless as possible. Relationships require sacrifice. If you are in a relationship with someone who does not understand why cheating is wrong or says that they can't help themselves then you should end it. If you are in a relationship with someone who says they are sorry and yet they keep cheating on you, you should know that they are not sorry. Being sorry denotes that you regret doing something. A person who cheats and says they are sorry may be telling the truth, but if they do it again, then obviously they didn't truly regret it the first time otherwise they would've known not to do it again.

Now would be a good time to address relationships that grow from infidelity; for example, if you cheated on your girlfriend and ended up dating the other girl. This relationship would be like a tree with shallow roots. The slightest storm would knock it over. Your relationship would probably be too weak to survive arguments and tough situations. Your relationship probably wouldn't be able to handle everything that came in its way. Anyone looking to destroy your relationship out of jealousy or envy could easily do so. Why? Because a relationship rooted in infidelity has no trust to reinforce it. You cannot trust someone who is known for cheating on people who they claimed to love. It will always be on the partners' mind that the same thing will happen to them. Not only that but a lot of people believe that what goes around comes around so they will always be thinking that since they took someone out of a relationship, they too will lose their relationship to someone else. This is a weak, unhealthy relationship that needs constant attention and more often than not, isn't worth the time and energy.

Actually, I wish I would've waited to write this chapter. Everything I've written before this paragraph, I wrote before my friend was cheated on. However things have changed, and someone I know personally and care for deeply has been cheated on. Which is okay, it's helped him to grow, and the insight he got from it has helped him learn tremendous things, and he's been more than helpful to me. I've developed some thoughts on everything though. First of all, she was being selfish, plain and simple, no two ways about it. That's all I can tell myself to help me understand. It's a hard concept for me to wrap my head around still. I've never been tempted to cheat, and if I was I wouldn't even dare to go through with it. I never could've imagined forgiving someone for cheating. I never could've imagined that he would forgive her for cheating on him. I never could've imagined him doing anything but hating her for it.

Then it happened. I couldn't understand, he told me "All I wanted to do was hold her and tell her that I'd always love her no matter what. All I wanted to do was take her shame away, take her guilt away; all I wanted to do was work things out. She's still God's princess. She's still the same girl she always was, she just made a mistake. Who hasn't made a mistake? Do I have too much pride that I'd be too hurt to try and work things out?"

Here's what I think though. I think she made a mistake. I think we've all made mistakes. I think she's young and has a lot of growing to do. I think she feels more guilt and shame than I will ever feel in my entire life. I think if she had to do it all over again she never would. All of those things comfort me. But nothing more than what I am about to say.

She betrayed him. It hurt him. At first, I think how could anyone betray someone they love like that? Then mid-sentence I realize something, something that changes everything. I betray. I have betrayed. I will always betray. Every time I sin, every time I think something I shouldn't be thinking, every time I spend another day alive, I betray Him. I betray God. I betray someone who has always been there and will always be there for me. I betray someone who has infinite unconditional love for me.

So who am I to think that I am too worthy to be betrayed?! How foolish of me. Shame on me. Forgive me for judging you. I'm sorry. Forgive me for the foolishness and animosity earlier in this chapter.

If someone you love cheats on you even though they love you, it's worth it to work things out. I've gone online, looking for advice. You'll see things like "once a cheater always a cheater." Or see other things trying to justify cheating. Or find things that will tell you, you obviously weren't passionate enough or giving her/him enough attention. I have even seen things that say cheating is good for relationships/marriages (Just another demonstration on how screwed up our culture is and how much damage we do to each other by distributing such ridiculous advice).There are no good excuses for cheating. The best reason to have is to have no idea why you did it. It's slightly more understandable. If you're a Christian who has been cheated on by another Christian and you want to understand why, here are a few passages from the bible. Galatians 5:17 says, "For the sinful nature desires what is contrary to the Spirit, and the Spirit what is contrary to the sinful nature. They are in conflict with each other, so that you do not do what you want." This would explain Romans 7:19 which says, "For what I do is not the good I want to do; no, the evil I do not want to do—this I keep on doing."

So what am I saying? I'm saying whoever cheated on you was under spiritual attack whether you like it or not. They do not need you to bring guilt or shame on them. Conviction comes from God. Continue to do the right thing. Be there for your partner and work through things with her. She is a victim of sin. Love her; do not hate her for being misled by evil. Eve was the first, and she walked with God and had everything, and still was misled. Adam too fell for the craftiness of Satan. You and I are no different and neither is the cheating partner. Be there for them. They need you now. You're supposed to depend on each other for the hard times, so be a man, and do what you're called to do.

Pornography

Pornography is something my household seldom talked about when I was growing up. When I was around eleven years old I would sneak off in the woods with my friend Albert and flip through a porn magazine that a girl down the street had stolen from her father for us. It was awesome (back then). And I never thought anything was morally wrong about it.

I'm not the only one who has felt this way about porn. Many people still do. How popular is pornography these days? Well, I've been researching it online. I've found a few interesting figures worth sharing. I feel like it says a lot about our society and where we place sexual gratification on our list of priorities.

- "Every second—$3,075.64 is being spent on pornography." [1]
- "Every second—28,258 internet users are viewing pornography." [2]

- "Every second—372 internet users are typing adult search terms into search engines."[3]
- "Every 39 minutes: a new pornographic video is being created in the United States."[4]
- "The average age at which men first see *Playboy* or a similar magazine is 11."[5]
- "25% of total search engine requests are porn-related."[6]
- "12% of total websites are pornographic"[7]
- "Child pornography generates $3 billion annually"[8]
- "20% of men admit accessing pornography at work"[9]
- "10% of adults admit having internet sexual addiction"[10]

That's just a few facts, there are tons more, but I think you get the idea.

Turns out, there is something wrong with being a part of this porn industry after all. Actually, until I was about eighteen (last year) I hadn't considered that there might be anything wrong with indulging every once in a while, or even every day. But to put it honestly, porn is a disastrous thing. Like all things it leaves you wanting more. Watch porn enough and you will want more. We always want more. Because when we get more, it becomes the normal amount and no longer satisfies like it used to, so we want even more. We see this in life. Given enough money, we will want more. Given enough fun, we will want more, given enough drugs, we will want more, given enough free time, and we will want more.

Given enough of anything we will want more. Porn is no different. First is soft core, and then we watch enough that it becomes normal, and no longer satisfies. So we move onto something else, perhaps hardcore, then, perhaps bondage. It could even go onto gay porn or incest or rape fantasies, anything to get to another level of heightened stimulus. The cycle does not stop. It only gets worse. It is important to recognize this and realize that porn is wrong. After a while, it will invade your relationship with your partner. It also sets unrealistic expectations for your partner. We see this in life, we watch movies filled with romance, we want romance, we watch actors always being happy, and we want to always be happy. If you watch porn, you are performing a grave injustice to your partner, if you love her enough, porn can be easily abolished. Porn should also be taken out of your life for the same reasons you shouldn't check out women or flirt with girls or cheat on your girlfriend. If you love her more than your lust for porn, it is your duty to prove it, not only for her, but for yourself. For porn will gradually ruin your relationship and taint your love.

I've heard stories from trusted sources. Stories of men who sleep with their lives and then when their wife goes to sleep they go and watch porn (sometimes in the same room as their wife). I've heard stories of men who can't have sex with their wife or don't want to and would rather watch porn. This is how dangerous it can be to watch porn and how much it can affect your relationships. Porn addiction is a common reason for many divorces. Don't end up like these men.

There are other things that should be mentioned from the story as well. A girl from down the street was giving us porn from her father. What does this tell us? This girl clearly knew that her father had porn; growing up in a household that pretended like there was nothing wrong with pornography, a household that openly shared pornography. How do you think this affected the girl? This girl, from a young age was being told that she had to act like the girls in the magazine, she was being told that sex and being sexy and being a whore would get her the attention she deserved. That's how she thought she had to gain approval in society. Porn was invading her life all because her father was addicted to it and brought it into his house and left it for his children to see.

What does God say about Porn? Nothing. Well, not directly anyway but he does give us instruction for how to live and behave. The following is some scripture and short explanations for how we can relate it to porn.

Mathew 5:27-28, "You have heard that it was said, 'Do not commit adultery.' But I tell you that anyone who looks at a woman lustfully has already committed adultery with her in his heart." This is Jesus talking and he states very simply that anyone looking at a woman sexually has committed adultery in his heart. Adultery is sex between a husband and woman who is not his wife or sex between a wife and a man who is not her husband. So when we watch porn do we look at women lustfully? Without a doubt. Does Jesus say this is wrong? Yes.

Proverbs 21:2 says, "All a man's ways seem right to him, but the LORD weighs the heart." In other words, you aren't fooling anybody. No matter how much you justify watching porn, God knows the truth. Even if you made yourself believe that watching porn was okay, God would know the truth to why you were really doing it.

James 1:13, "When tempted, no one should say, "God is tempting me." For God cannot be tempted by evil, nor does he tempt anyone; but each one is tempted when, by his own evil desire, he is dragged away and enticed. Then, after desire has conceived, it gives birth to sin; and sin, when it is full-grown, gives birth to death."

This one is pretty simple, temptation does not come from God but from the evil, giving into temptation (i.e. watching porn) is the same as giving in to evil.

Ephesians 5:3-4 is a great verse because I think it can be directly interpreted for teachings about pornography, "But among you there must not be even a hint of sexual immorality, or of any kind of impurity, or of greed, because these are improper for God's holy people. Nor should there be obscenity, foolish talk or coarse joking, which are out of place, but rather thanksgiving." I think "obscenity" is a great synonym for porn. After all, doesn't porn usually if not always contain obscenity? Isn't porn impure? Isn't it true that as God's people we should have nothing to do with this?

2 Corinthians 7:1 "Since we have these promises, dear friends, let us purify ourselves from everything that contaminates body and spirit, perfecting holiness out of reverence for God." Obviously, we have proven a number of times that pornography makes our soul unclean, as it is giving into temptation and giving into Satan. So by doing so we are not even coming close to making an effort to perfecting holiness.

Hebrews 13:4 "Marriage should be honored by all, and the marriage bed kept pure, for God will judge the adulterer and all the sexually immoral." This verse could easily apply to the unmarried as well because you will probably one day get married and you should respect your future wife the same way you should respect your current wife. Therefore, even if we aren't married we should still remain faithful for the woman that we haven't met yet. And some people who engage in the pornography you are watching maybe be married, the whole industry fights against honoring marriage and therefore fights against God. That isn't something you should want to be a part of.

2 Timothy 2:22 says, "Flee the evil desires of youth, and pursue righteousness, faith, love and peace, along with those who call on the Lord out of

a pure heart." I think the last part of this verse is very crucial: "along with those who call on the Lord out of a pure heart." I think it's important to recognize that if we have people who we can talk to about our temptations, people who will encourage us, if we have people who we can depend on for help and guidance, then things will be much easier. Because giving up porn can definitely be a struggle.

1 Thessalonians 4:2-3 "For you know what instructions we gave you by the authority of the Lord Jesus. It is God's will that you should be sanctified: that you should avoid sexual immorality" I love this verse. God wants you to be holy and completely free from sexual immorality. Why? He loves us. He wants what's best for us. He knows that our lives will be more complete if we are free from sexual immortality.

So God never once mentions pornography. Perhaps because if God was extremely specific about everything we should or shouldn't do it would take too much time to read and it would also take away from the main focus of the bible. But from God's word it is not a far stretch to make the connection of lust and evil thinking with porn and after you do that it is easy to see Gods instruction on porn.

You may think to yourselves, "How the heck am I going to stop from checking out girls and flirting with girls and cheating on girls and watching pornography, when I've been doing it for so long." It's true, it is hard to stop doing all of these things once they've become habit, once they've become engrained in your mind as something totally fine. Part of the reason it has gotten this far, is because most of these things are socially acceptable in society. Society fuels it and wants us to want it. The commercial industry is glad that we have sexual desires and tries to feed our sexual desires in order to sell. So it is understandable to think there is no way out, or to think that I am asking for too much, but the truth is... you can condition yourself to act in a virtuous way. For example, how many of you kill a person every Friday night? Hopefully not many of you. Why? Because you know that killing a person is wrong. Well, you now know that checking out women is wrong, so why can't you stop? Maybe because killing people is a disgusting thing to do. Well, why not condition yourself to think that porn is disgusting and filthy and unrighteous? You can. It isn't hard. Just tell yourself that porn is filthy and reinforce it in your mind. And take away all the conditioning that society has put you through.

I think it's easy to become addicted to pornography. I haven't watched it in almost two years and I don't ever plan on watching it again. If you think you struggle with an addiction then you should take it seriously and maybe even seek additional help. XXXchurch.com has plenty of resources for helping Christians with porn addictions and if you feel like you need extra help in your struggle, then I would definitely point you in that direction.

Please respect the one you love. Do not take her for granted. Love her the way she deserves. Do not give into temptation; do not allow your lust for others to grow. Instead, feed your love for your partner. Allow your love to grow. If you have a problem, do something to correct it; don't let your pride stand in the way of having a strong loving relationship.

Do not be foolish in life. Foolishness is the opposite of wisdom. Wisdom is what separates a man from being a child. Love demands wisdom.

Sex

Let's talk about sex. Sex is most definitely a good thing. I don't think anyone could say that sex is a bad thing. Sex is definitely something that one should get to experience, unless of course, they didn't want to. Sex is not a necessity. It is something we could easily live without. We aren't stupid creatures that need to give into our desires in order to be happy. We aren't beasts that need to have sex in order to be healthy. Such things do not exist.

Before we go any further, I'd like to look at some sex facts and how the world/America feels about it. These are some facts I've found online.

- Impotence is grounds for divorce in 26 U.S. states.[1]
- Oral sex is on the rise amongst 12-14 year olds in the US and most believe that it is not in fact a sexual practice[2]
- Chances that an American man believes that oral sex does not constitute adultery: 1 in 8[3]

- Chance that an American woman believes that oral sex does not constitute adultery: 1 in 9[4]
- Percentage of Americans who believe that "adultery can sometimes be good for a marriage": 22[5]
- Percentage of newlyweds who say they consummated their relationship on the first date: 17 [6]
- The U.S. has the highest rate of teen pregnancy, birth, and abortion in the industrialized world.[7]

There are plenty more, but that's a good start. Now, please read further to see another view point that many other men share with me that shows sex in a somewhat different light.

I would advise you to not have sex until you are married. Sex is a very sacred thing and although it is undoubtedly good, the longer you wait the better it will be and the less you do it, the better it will be. Like eating junk food, eat a lot of it and you will get a tummy ache and won't really care for it anymore. However if you eat it rarely it stays a delicacy.

Also, if done under the wrong conditions, it will have more negative affects than positive.

But of course, that isn't the only reason for waiting for sex, that wouldn't be good enough for me. Besides, that is a selfish reason in the first place. The best reason that I could give to wait for sex is, of course, is in the name of love. More than anyone in the world, you should love your wife. Well, perhaps equal to your children. Or love your children more, I have no idea. But anyway, more to the point: Love your wife. And a great gesture of love for your wife...the greatest I would be able to think of is to wait to lose your virginity to her.

Imagine waiting until you got married. Imagine all the girls you meet from the time you start thinking about having sex to the time you get married. Imagine being able to say to your wife, "out of all the girls in the world, out of every girl I have ever seen and could ever imagine, you are the one that I want to have sex with, I saved this for you." Also imagine your wife being able to walk around the world and never have to meet a person who has also had sex with her husband.

Imagine it the other way around. Imagine getting married and having someone in your office say "yeah, I had that before." Certainly it would feel better to know that no one would be able to say that about your wife, that no other guy would ever touch her in the same ways that you have. What a great thing to be able to share with each other.

The phrase "true love waits" is some what obnoxious, I will agree. It is as if those who wait are better than those who don't, or as if those who wait love more than those who don't. This is simply wrong; those who don't wait are equally capable of loving just as much as those who do wait until marriage to have sex.

I'm not saying that if you don't wait to have sex until marriage, that you don't love your partner. I'm simply saying that it is a huge way to show your love and it is a very special thing to share together, a very intimate and special and private act. Also, part of the reason people don't wait is lack of knowledge or lack of perspective.

I would be doing you a very grave injustice if I stopped there. There is a problem with having sex outside of marriage. It is not as good as waiting to have sex until marriage. It is better to wait until marriage to have sex.

The people that choose this path may not be better people. They may not be better husbands and their love may not be stronger. Waiting until marriage does not necessarily mean that you are a better person and I would never pretend that it does. But the benefits of waiting until marriage do far outweigh the benefits of not waiting. The reason

I make this distinction is because I do not want people to feel like I am placing judgment or that I am looking down on them in anyway.

CAUTION: reading the following text will challenge your ideas and values. New insight may cause you to take responsibility for your actions. You may need to correct the way you're used to doing things. You may need to stop doing some things all together. You may get angry or you may feel regret. Please read this text if you want to become a better boyfriend.

God made us so that sex was necessary for our survival. Not only that but God made sex pleasurable to us, to such an extent that nothing else compares to it. God made man, and took one good look at him and said "it is not good for man to be alone." God wants us to have sex and to find good pleasure within sex. He wants us to "be fruitful and multiply." He wants us to be with women.

Satan has no desire to lead us into sexual fulfillment. Only by following God's will can we find sex to be as fulfilling as we expect it to be. God is the designer of sex; he knows a lot more than a Cosmopolitan magazine does when it comes to having sex and making the most of it. I have heard a lot of people tell me that sex is not what they thought it would be. A lot of frustrated girls thinking that sex would be this amazing, incomparable experience only to find that they are extremely disappointed.

Sex is more than just a physical experience. The bible says that it is a merging of two people's souls. The bible says sex is a unity of flesh. Even a non-Christian can see this. When someone is raped, the pain experienced is horrible and tragic. When someone gets there hand cut off, even they do not feel the pain equivalent to that of a rape victim. This is because sex is far more than a physical thing. And rape is far more than a physical pain. If sex was purely physical, with no emotions involved, than raping someone would equate to beating someone. But this is not the case. Rape is far worse. Why? And why do we know this but yet we continue running around and acting like sex is just a physical experience between two people? Why is it crammed into television shows and movies that sex is nothing more than exercise that feels good?

Sex is a combination of spiritual, mental and physical meshing. Therefore sex should never be casual. And should be reserved for someone special, someone you want to spend the rest of your life with.

Sex before marriage will give you memories and knowledge that have nothing to do with your life, that have no context or meaning in your life. It will be a waste when you finally have a husband. And you could possibly both carry the guilt of having been with another person. Of course you will act like it doesn't matter, you will say you are glad you had sex with someone because it would've been awkward if you were a virgin and your husband wasn't or something like that. And your husband will avoid the conversation too. And you will probably teach your children that it's okay to have sex before marriage. I've seen this pretty often. Parents telling their kids to have sex, it's like if they can teach it as a good thing, it will turn into a good thing, or the more people they can get to join them, the less bad they will feel about it, because everyone is doing it.

For the people that say that sex is not what they thought it would be, for the people that were disappointed with the sex they had, this is because they weren't having sex for the purpose that it was intended for. They were misusing sex.

Sex is an act of inward love. You will never have fulfillment from sex until you have it the way God wants you to. If you gave a present to someone but you didn't really like them, then you wouldn't get as much out of it as you would have if you really loved them and really wanted them to have a present. You could give someone a thousand presents and you wouldn't feel good about it, it wouldn't make you happy and it wouldn't make you like that person. You must like them first and then you give them a present. Just like it doesn't matter how many times you have sex, it will never feel like what it was meant to feel like unless you love your partner. That's not to say that emotions won't still play a factor, it's just to say that sex won't be as fulfilling as it was designed to be.

So you can have sex over and over again and you won't get fulfillment from it unless you feel it in your heart first. Casual sex with strangers or friends or boyfriends/girlfriends will never be as fulfilling as sex with your husband, or wife.

Sex outside of marriage is not an act of love if you know the consequences of your actions. I do not want to have sex with my girlfriend, because I love her so much that I would not want to hurt her, so even if she does end up marrying someone else, I want her to be happy. And I want her husband to be happy and I don't want to take anything away from them that they deserve to be able to share only between each other. Some people say, well what if you know you are going to marry your girlfriend? I would say to them, the longer you wait the better it will be, I would say to them, it's better to play it safe, I would say to them, if you loved your girlfriend you would wait as long as you had to, finally I would say that if you loved your girlfriend you would make sure you were married so you wouldn't have to worry about hurting her or taking something that she would've wanted to save for her husband. And so she wouldn't have to worry that you might leave her after having had sex and justifying it by saying "we'll definitely get married." Then, she'll always be thinking, "What if we don't?"

It takes a lot more love to not have sex then it does to have sex. Sex outside of marriage takes that which is deeply personal and makes it general and generic. It makes it normal and not as special as it was intended to be. We talk about making our love more valuable, well you can also lower the value of your sex by having sex without discretion. Sex with a prostitute means nothing because they have sex with everyone, so you wouldn't feel loved and it wouldn't come anywhere close to feeling as good as sex the way it was designed.

Sex outside of marriage puts a huge weight on us.

That weight is guilt. And the last thing I want to do is have my girlfriend walking around with that much guilt in her life. Damaging another human being is never an act of love.

I hope that from reading this. You will be able to have fulfilling, God-intended sex because it is the best way to have sex. It is the only way that sex will feel as good as you expect it to.

So what about doing things other than sex? Certainly we can do sexual acts without having vaginal intercourse. There is a plethora of things that we can do with girls that isn't considered sex. So how do we know what is right and what isn't? How do we know when we've crossed the line or how do we know what our limits are?

I think it's good to draw a line somewhere so that you can be more obedient to staying in the parameters of a healthy relationship. I also think it's good to know the reasons for establishing these lines. It's a tricky subject.

I think it's easier to simplify things so over the years I have come to determine that the best way to decide how to behave around your girlfriend as far as sexual pleasures are concerned is by following two simple rules.

The first rule is, don't do anything with your

girlfriend that you wouldn't want your future wife to be doing. In other words, if you wouldn't want your future wife to give someone "hand jobs" than you shouldn't expect hand jobs. I think if we were all honest, we would want our wives to have done nothing sexual at all. So it would only be fair if you were to support your girlfriend and tell her that you don't want to do anything sexually with her. See the trust chapter for the advantages of not being sexually active.

The other rule for deciding what you should do with girls is to only do what you would want your daughter to be doing. In other words, if you don't want your daughter to be giving people hand jobs than you should respect your girlfriends father and encourage her not to be sexual with you or anybody else until she's ready.

If you doubt doing something or if you put it into question whether or not you should do something, it is always safer to just wait until marriage. That's the best advice I could give you.

Don't Date?

So, you shouldn't have sex until you're married, you shouldn't do anything sexual with anyone until you're married, you shouldn't develop a physical relationship with anyone until you're married, should you even consider being in a relationship?

That depends. If your idea of a relationship necessitates sexual actions then you should probably hold off on a relationship. But then again, if you've gotten this far into the book and you still feel that fulfilling sexual desires has to be part of a relationship then you have either been reading without thinking or I've done a terrible job writing this book.

That being said, it's extremely important to be in relationships before you get married (for most people). Marrying your spouse is the most important decision you will ever make in your entire life. Deciding who you're going to be with for the rest of your life takes time, testing, and patience. I would say it's almost necessary to have a relationship with someone or even a few someones before you decide to get married. Don't get me wrong if you meet the right girl and she happens to be the only girl you've ever dated, then by all means you should keep her and never give her up and don't look for something better. If she is what makes you happy, then you have no need to date anyone else, and it is of no importance whatsoever. As a matter of fact, if that is the case than what you really need to do is be sure to never date anyone else, as long as she makes you happy and treats you right and wants to be with you. Not right in the sense of today's standards but treats you like you aught to be treated, as outlined in the book. Same goes for women.

But how should this look? This "I'm you're boyfriend, you're my girlfriend" experience. Should you hug? Should you hold hands? Should you kiss? Should you make out? Should you have other forms of sex as long as it isn't vaginal? Should you do what adults would call "petting? Or groping or "feeling each other up?" Should you be naked in front of each other?

Well, not everything is outlined perfectly for us, and if it were, then we'd be able to find loopholes and justify the things we really wanted to do, wouldn't we? We can justify just about anything with these great minds we've been given.

As far as relationships go, I think it is wisest to concentrate on being someones best friend. Many marriages are built from lust, from fulfilling each others sexual desires to the point that all the other factors of a relationship are overshadowed. These people then get older and less attracted to each other physically, and they lose what first sustained their relationship enough to keep it above water and now they begin to sink. They begin to realize how much they don't have in common, how different their beliefs and morals are, or even that there personalities don't match enough to keep each other happy and entertained. Maybe one gets bored of the other. Maybe one gets annoyed by the others' mannerisms. We have an increasing divorce rate. This is one major factor. You want to have a happy marriage; the best way is to start preparing for it before you're married.

So please, I beg you, build relationships. Find someone you can love. You know that "best friend" stage that so many guys are afraid of getting into, because they think they won't be able to crawl out of it and be her "boyfriend?." Well that's exactly what our culture wants us to believe will happen. But in reality, being a best friend is the large part of what it means to be her husband, and being her best friend should be the entire part of what it means to be her boyfriend. So be her best friend. Learn everything you can about each other. Take care of each other, watch out for one another, and focus on that and nothing else. If you really want something outlined in black and white, then first of all I'd say focus on what you feel is right, based on the other chapters. If you don't want to be the guy that saw someone else's wife naked before they did, then don't be that guy. Respect your girlfriend. Love her, and protect her from hurting herself and her future marriage.

What about kissing, hugging and holding hands? Best friends do that. Jesus himself would hold your hand and hug and kiss you if you wanted him to. He let a potential prostitute wash his feet with her hair. I think he'd give you a peck on the cheek. Last time I checked parents kiss their children and hug them all the time. Boys in Africa hold hands as a sign of friendship. It's all good.

Is that even possible? How could we ever conceive of being someones boyfriend or girlfriend without making out with them and pleasuring them physically and without the connection that comes along with physically pleasuring each other?

Well first of all, that bond that we seek, we should only seek that with the person we are married to. Second of all, I know people who have dated their husbands and wives for years without even kissing them on the lips. As a matter of fact my brother hasn't kissed his fiancé since they've started dating. So don't think it can't be done. And don't think that it isn't worth a try. And don't think you can't do it. Those are simply cop outs. And if you think you're showing more love by "needing" sexual pleasures from you're girlfriend, you're not. You're showing her less love. You're taking something from her that you have absolutely no right to take. As a matter of fact, sex and sexual actions aren't what make us love somebody, the love comes first. So don't think that you will love someone more or that they will love you more after you've done something physical, it won't change anything because it doesn't work that way.

So what will make your relationship with your boyfriend or girlfriend any different from your relationship with your close friends or siblings? First of all, don't be afraid of a title. Be proud of a title. Don't be afraid of being labeled someones boyfriend or girlfriend from the connotations that come with the labels. Make your own connotations. Second of all, you're trying to get to know as much about one another as you possibly can. You're loving that person as much as you can. You're caring for one another as much as you can. And you're also saying to that person, that they've got potential. So much potential that you want to give them a chance, more so than anyone else you know. And by labeling each other and calling each other boyfriend and girlfriend, other people will know that you're serious about each other and hopefully they will respect that and not try to hurt your relationship. You also get a sense of security, which is a big deal to many people. Parents love their kids more than they love other people's kids, but they don't need to show it in some specific way, so when you love your girlfriend more than your other friends, you too don't need some physical act to show it. You know it, they know it, and other people will know it.

So have girlfriends and boyfriends, love each other, spend time with each other, be her best friend, so you can know whether or not you're right to marry each other, and then when the time comes, you will have put all the time and effort and patience into making the strongest marriage you could've ever conceived of. Why want anything less? It's beautiful.

I'd also like to bring up another point from an earlier chapter. That is, being in a relationship with someone that you know you couldn't possibly ever want to marry. The question is, why do such a thing? Why would you have such a temporary meaningless relationship? What could possibly be the point of it, outside of physical desires? I suppose you do get a sense of security from it, you probably even get some emotional joy out of it, although there is room for pain as well. But aren't you cheating yourself? Aren't you selling yourself short to date someone that you know you won't marry? Don't you and the other person deserve more than that? Isn't it a bit selfish to ask a person to settle for less when you know they deserve more? Please, don't waste your time and don't devalue your love by acting so carelessly with it. Take care of yourself, treat yourself with respect, demand what you deserve and don't sell yourself short. Please.

MASTURBATION

Masturbation is an extremely controversial subject among Christians and has been highly debated for many years. Therefore, I'm not going to tell you what is right or wrong or whether you should or should not masturbate. Rather, I am going to give you pros and cons of masturbation. I will explain each one thoroughly and let you come to your own conclusion about whether or not the pros and cons are legitimate. From there, you can weigh out the pros and cons against one another and eventually decide for yourself whether masturbation is good or bad.

My friends and I had a bible study on this once. We started out by listing all the pros of masturbating and all of the cons.

Possible Pros:

- Sexual Pleasure
- Stress Reliever

- Escape from Reality
- Decreases Sexual Urge

Possible Cons:

- Implicit Adultery
- Unhealthy Comparison of Fictional Girls to Real Girls
- Desensitization (Mentally and Sexually)
- Possible Cause of Premature Ejaculation
- Guilt
- Addictive
- Can Destroy Relationships
- Selfish
- Gateway for Pornography
- Conditions Your Body to Become More Sexually Responsive to Masturbation

Let's start by discussing the pros. The first pro we named was sexual pleasure. Certainly it's easy to see how masturbating can be sexually stimulating. I don't think it needs any further explanation than that. The second pro was a stress reliever, for some, masturbation is used to relieve stress just like lifting weights or jogging. The third pro was "escape from reality." In other words, when we masturbate we can use fictional stories for stimulation and so for the brief time that we are masturbating, we don't have to worry about what's going on in our lives. The last pro is a decrease in sexual urge. What I meant by that is some people masturbate so they can not be so horny during the rest of the day. For example, I have a friend, and every time he feels an urge to have sex with his girlfriend, he will masturbate so he is no longer horny. That way he has less temptation when he is with her. That's all pretty easy to understand I think so now we'll move on to the cons.

The first con we listed was "possible implicit adultery." In other words, when we masturbate sometimes we think about other girls besides our girlfriends or our wives or whatever. Basically, you're fantasizing about other women and you should never do that. If you would like more information on why we shouldn't fantasize about other women you can go to the chapters: "Checking Out" girls and Flirting, Cheating and or Pornography.

The second con was "Unhealthy Comparison of Fictional girls to Real Girls." In other words when you masturbate, you could be thinking about girls like models or porn stars or just any girls in general. This would lead to an unhealthy comparison because you would start to feel like all girls should look like the ones you fantasize about. Or perhaps you would simply become less attracted to certain girls because you would be comparing them to girls that you fantasize about subconsciously.

The third con was mental and sexual desensitization. In other words you would become less mentally and sexually sensitive to the content that you masturbated to. We talked about this a little in the pornography chapter. But to recap, if you were to start out by watching soft core porn, you would get used to seeing those pictures or videos and eventually you would become less stimulated by it. You would end up wanting to watch hard core porn or something different and more extreme. This can also be dangerous because lets say you've been masturbating or looking at porn all your life. Well when you finally get married you could be less attracted to your wife due to all of the desensitization that you have put your mind through. That is unfair to your wife and to you. You should be able to have the chance to appreciate the beauty of your wife completely. So desensitization could be a serious con for masturbation.

Another con to masturbating is possible premature ejaculation. The reasoning for this is that masturbating conditions your penis to ejaculate as soon as possible. After all, the main reason that people masturbate is so that they can get the physical pleasure of ejaculating. So you try to make yourself ejaculate as soon as possible. This is bad because when it comes time to have sex with your wife or pleasure your wife, you will not be able to live up to your potential because of all the time you have spent conditioning your body to ejaculate sooner and sooner.

The fifth con for masturbating that we listed was "guilt." In other words, if you had decided that masturbating was wrong, than it would cause a lot of guilt if you kept doing it even though you had at one point decided it was wrong.

The next con of masturbating was that it is addictive. It's an extremely easy thing for guys to do and it provides an extremely high amount of pleasure and therefore it can be very psychologically addictive. This is bad because once you're addicted it will be harder for you to stop and you could easily cause any of the other cons to happen.

The seventh con that we listed was that masturbating can destroy your relationships. This is obviously dependent on the other cons. But nonetheless it is still a con and shouldn't be ignored.

Another con for masturbating is selfishness. Masturbation is an act done for you. The only purpose to masturbating is to bring sexual pleasure. Masturbation conditions you to become selfish when being sexual because you concentrate on your own satisfaction and this could pour over to times when you're having sex, not just masturbating.

The second to last con was opening a gateway to pornography. In other words, if you masturbate, chances are you will want to use porn to stimulate your senses. We have already discussed the problems of pornography in the related chapter and it is a bad thing therefore increasing your temptation to watch porn is an obvious con.

The last con is that masturbation conditions your body to become more responsive to masturbation and the fantasies that go with it. In other words, the brain associates sexual pleasure with masturbation over and over again every time you do it. This could actually cause you to like masturbation more than you would like having sex. Many wives are left feeling neglected because of this.

So now you have all the pros and cons that I could think of for masturbation and you have all the explanations of them. It's up to you whether you decide it is right or wrong. I would suggest that you feel free to do your own research or meet with trusted church officials or trusted adults that you and others consider wise and see what they think about what you've read and what your thoughts are. Make sure to get many well-rounded perspectives and feel free to bring this book with you and discuss the pros and cons.

The bible says absolutely nothing about masturbation. It does give directions on lust which are in the other chapters but it doesn't have anything to say concerning masturbation.

One Christian perspective on masturbation is that sin is something that alienates us from God, and since masturbation is focused completely on the self, it does not bring us closer to God and it does not help us love others so if we become absorbed in masturbation, if it becomes a big part of your life than it will become a sin. So from a Christian perspective you should decide for yourself whether or not masturbation is a sin. And again, I would urge you to talk to church counselors or pastors for guidance and advice.

Drug Abuse

This chapter may not seem like it has much to do with relationships. But all throughout high school and middle school, I hear people justify drugs and I know people getting drunk and getting high but trying to live moral lives and thinking that their actions are harmless. They aren't, and they can affect your relationships.

Drugs are not uncommon. Even in middle school many people are doing drugs. Many people don't know why they shouldn't be doing drugs; it's an easy way to make them feel good. Or they know some of the reasons but it isn't enough to make them stop. Which is understandable; drugs are addictive after all. However if you can't give up drugs for a relationship, you shouldn't be in one. Relationships are about sacrifice. If you can't give up something like drugs to make your relationship better, than the reasons for you being in a relationship have to do with fulfilling your own passions. This is not a healthy, loving relationship. Most of the time people aren't willing to give up drugs because they don't see why it's so bad to do them in the first place.

Part of the reason why the people who do drugs don't see why it's wrong is because if they did see why it was wrong; they would feel obligated to give it up. So it's easier not to think about the consequences of drugs abuse.

First of all, I'd like to start by saying that people only do things that make their lives better. Or rather, they only do things that they think will make their lives better. This is true from what I've experienced in my life. Even if someone attempts to commit suicide, they do this because they think life is too hard and they will be better off dead. People work out to lose weight. People watch TV to laugh. People don't work out so they have time to relax. People don't watch TV because they want to be more active. Whatever people are doing they do it because they feel it will be good for them, not bad for them. No one does something that is bad for them. Even a person who gives away everything he owns is doing it because he thinks it will make him a better person, or he's doing it because if he didn't he'd feel bad. Whatever the reason is, and whatever the thing is, people are doing it to make their lives better.

So now I'd like to ask you, if you are doing drugs or plan to do drugs, does it really make your life better? For those of you who take drugs for medicinal use, the answer is yes, it does make your life better overall. For those of you who use drugs for recreational use, I would urge you to answer this question honestly.

Is your drug use coming in between you and the ones you love? What I mean by this is do you feel obligated to hide this part of your life from someone, from a family member or a girlfriend? Do you ever argue about your drug use with the people that do know? Do you distance yourself or spend less time with certain people just because they don't do drugs? The problem with hiding part of your life from a family member is that it creates space between the two of you. You can't have an open and honest relationship. Are drugs more important than your relationships? Even if your girlfriend said she didn't care about you drinking or using drugs, it could still be affecting your relationship. Part of this is trust, when you aren't doing drugs, or putting yourself in tempting situations, it's much easier for your partner to trust your decision making skills, but there is more to it than just trust. Another thing to point out is that when you're drunk you aren't completely your true self. You act a little differently, and I know at least for myself, I like to have genuine relationships with the people I date and never desire them to be any different of act any differently. I have friends who only hang out with people when they're drunk because they're more fun that way. I would hate to think that anyone out there is like that toward someone they're in a serious relationship with. It's probably not the case. Most would probably agree that spending time together while you're both your normal selves is much more rewarding than being under the influence of drugs.

Is your drug use decreasing your physical and mental health? If it isn't for medicinal use, then the answer is yes. This all goes back to not taking your life for granted. You have been given something special and you only get one shot at it, do you really want to ruin it with drug use just because you're bored on the weekends or its fun to do? Certainly there are other things you can do that are just as fun.

Drugs will always have a negative impact, so you must decide for yourself whether or not the advantages of taking drugs weigh out the disadvantages. If you are in love, I would advise you not to do recreational drugs. You wouldn't want your poor lifestyle habits to affect hers. And if she and you already did drugs before the two of you met, I would still advise you to stop so that you can better protect her from the negative impact of drugs. After all, how can you expect her to quit when you're still doing it. And why would you want her to keep doing it if you know it is bad for her health.

You also don't have to hit rock bottom in order to reform. In most cases, the more time you spend trying to get rid of a drug addiction, the more likely you are to overcome it. And therefore you shouldn't actually wait until you hit rock bottom. You should start as soon as possible. Plus, the longer and longer you do drugs than the more and more addicted to them you become.

I'm also talking about getting drunk. You should show others that you don't have to drink in order to live a fulfilling life; you should show your friends and your girlfriend that drinking and partying isn't the right path. You should lead the ones you love away from the path of destruction. Drinking will cause you to lose important coping skills and instead of working your problems out in a healthy way, you will turn to a quick temporary fix of drinking. Is this what you want for your girlfriend? Drinking will also cause degenerative effects to your brain and organs. Is this what you want for your girlfriend? Drinking will lower your inhibitions and cause you to do things that you wouldn't normally do. Is this what you want for your girlfriend? If you don't straighten up then you can't expect your girlfriend to straighten up and it could mean tragedy for the ones you love or simply for the relationship you have.

Also if you can stop drinking then you can increase the trust that you and your partner have together. Your partner can see that you won't be put in compromising situations because you know how to lead yourself away temptation. Trust is a very important part of your relationship so if you can increase the amount of trust there is than you could make your relationship better so why not? How important is drinking?

What does the bible think about drinking and drugs use? Well, some people would tell you that marijuana is natural and if God didn't want us to smoke it than he wouldn't have made it. That's a lie and it's not very well thought out. I'd hate to address this but I feel like someone would take it seriously so here it goes. God loves us and he gave us free will. He doesn't advise us to use this free will anyway we like. 1 Corinthians 10:23 says "Everything is permissible, but not everything is beneficial. Everything is permissible, but not everything is constructive." So as you can see, just because we can do things, or just because some things exist doesn't mean we should do it.

What else does God say about getting drunk? A lot actually. Mostly it is about drinking and not other forms of drugs abuse, but I think we can acquire that God's reasoning for not getting drunk would be the same reasoning he'd give us for not getting high.

Proverbs 20:1
Wine is a mocker and beer a brawler;
whoever is led astray by them is not wise.

Ephesians 5:18
Do not get drunk on wine, which leads to debauchery.
Instead, be filled with the Spirit.

Galatians 5:16-17
So I say, live by the Spirit, and you will not gratify

the desires of the sinful nature. For the sinful nature desires what is contrary to the Spirit, and the Spirit what is contrary to the sinful nature. They are in conflict with each other, so that you do not do what you want.

Galatians 5:19-22
The acts of the sinful nature are obvious: sexual immorality, impurity and debauchery; 20idolatry and witchcraft; hatred, discord, jealousy, fits of rage, selfish ambition, dissensions, factions 21and envy; drunkenness, orgies, and the like. I warn you, as I did before, that those who live like this will not inherit the kingdom of God.

1 Thessalonians 5:6-10 says
So then, let us not be like others, who are asleep, but let us be alert and self-controlled. For those who sleep, sleep at night, and those who get drunk, get drunk at night. But since we belong to the day, let us be self-controlled, putting on faith and love as a breastplate, and the hope of salvation as a helmet. For God did not appoint us to suffer wrath but to receive salvation through our Lord Jesus Christ. He died for us so that, whether we are awake or asleep, we may live together with him.

So I think it's pretty obvious that God doesn't want us to get drunk or do drugs. One common reason for God not wanting us to do drugs is so that we will have a firm hold on reality. He does this because he loves us and knows that it is dangerous for us to become absorbed in a realm of fiction and fantasy. He knows that our thoughts and actions can easily be misconstrued by the effects of drugs. He wants us to be safe and to make responsible decisions.

Now I have to make something perfectly clear here. I had a friend call me up recently, asking me if I think she should go back on her medication. I told her I thought she should. The reason she has medication, the reason she needs medication is because she is chemically imbalanced. The drugs balance her, the way she was supposed to be. Then she disagreed. "How do you know I'm not supposed to be chemically imbalanced?" She asked. I said "Look, if someone is sick with a fever they take medicine; no one thinks less of them for having to take it. If someone is missing a limb, they use an artificial one; no one thinks less of them for having to take it."

I just wanted to make that clear, it's important to take medicine when you need it but don't take drugs when you don't need it.

Too Late?

So, now what happens if it's all too late? What happens if you didn't read the book in time and you've already made mistakes that you wish you hadn't made? Is it too late? Are there things you can do to redeem yourself?

The following chapter will cover these questions. Whether its porn or sex or masturbation or cheating on girls or whatever else we discussed. We'll cover all of it. We'll go in order one by one down the list of responsibilities and behaviors for a boyfriend.

Let's start with checking out girls and flirting. What if it's too late? Well, let's be honest, I've already done it several times, you've probably already done it several times. It's okay. It isn't the end of the world. The important thing is that we've realized it's wrong and that we need to change.

So what happens if we've committed to changing and we slip up? What happens if we are tempted to flirt and we give in, or we check girls out? Well, let's be honest it'll probably happen. You'll probably feel guilty or a little convicted, which is great. Just remember it isn't the end of the world, and you're not a bad person. The very fact that you feel conviction about it proves that you're a better person than most. It's hard to be perfect and we shouldn't expect to be. Strive to be like God but don't compete with God. Know that you aren't perfect. Ask God for help to make you better. Do not feel bad if you don't get it right the first few tries. Do not be frustrated if you keep messing up. When we first begin to walk our parents do not yell at us for falling down, they do not get upset with us and say "Why can't you walk, what's wrong with you?!" but rather they pick us back up and tell us to try again.

Next on the list is cheating. What happens if you've cheated before? Is it too late? Well, the "is it too late" question has two parts. Is it too late to salvage your old relationship and seek forgiveness and try to move on and love your girlfriend and not lose her? No it's never too late for that. Unless of course, she says it's too late. Don't become obsessed, listen to your girlfriend and respect her, give her space and time. Love her enough to be submissive to her will. The next question: is it too late to get a new girlfriend? No. If you've committed yourself to changing and if you want to uphold high moral values than, great for you. Everyone is capable of changing. Just because you've cheated doesn't mean you'll do it again.

What happens if you're committed to changing and slip up? What happens if you cheat again? If you just can't seem to help cheating on somebody than you need to read a different book or seek some therapeutic help.

Pornography, is it too late? It's never too late to stop looking at pornography; the sooner, the better. Is it bad that you did it? Yes. Is it understandable and forgivable? Yes. What if it happens again? The truth is, a lot of people struggle with it. Pastors, teachers, parents, it's a common thing. Even newly weds struggle with it. Even people who have been married for fifty years struggle with it. The truth is you can stop forever. But let's say that you messed up and committed to stopping but you faltered and watched porn again. Well it's good for you to feel convicted about this. If you're in a serious relationship than consider talking to your girlfriend or wife about your struggle. If you're afraid that you have an addiction, than seek extra help. But know that there are plenty of people in the same boat as you. Yes, pornography is disgusting but it's a hard thing to overcome. Expect it to take time and devotion.

Now, we have a good topic to address, sex. What happens if you've already had sex? Is it too late? It's never too late to stop having sex. Sure, you won't be a virgin anymore. But the less memories and experiences you have with sex outside of marriage, the better. It doesn't make sense that just because you don't have the most pure sexuality you should make it even worse. Or that you shouldn't strive to make it better. There are ways of making things better. For example, simply admonishing your old behavior and changing your lifestyle is a great start. Than at least you could say to your husband or boyfriends that you're a new person. You can tell them that ever since a certain point in time you have decided to change your ways and have had a new perspective on life.

Also if you're Christian you can ask God to take away your memories and feelings that are associated with your past. You can ask God for forgiveness and ask him to make you pure again. After all none of us are pure except through Christ's sacrifice. Only God can wash us clean. There's nothing that Christ's blood can't make pure including your sexual history. It's a hard concept to understand but perhaps after you've done it you'll have a fuller grasp and appreciation for God's power of forgiveness.

I also want to address something else, if you meet a girl and you really really like her and you may even love her and then you find out she's not a virgin, don't give up. Don't be one of those guys that says "I only want to marry a virgin." Don't be one of those guys who thinks to themselves "she's already had sex, she's not worthy enough for me." If you do think that way than the brutal honest truth is that you're not worthy enough for her. Plenty of people make mistakes when they're young, especially when they're brought up in this society. No one has the same past and therefore no one can look at another's life and say "I would've handled that situation differently."

Masturbation, Is it too late? No. It's never too late to stop masturbating, if that's what you've decided to do. It's also okay if you decide not to masturbate but fall back every once in a while. It's the same as porn. You should feel convicted about it, but you shouldn't obsess. It's a struggle for most men who decide not to do it. It's a hard thing to try and overcome. Like I said before, you'd already be better than most just by feeling convicted about it.

And now drug abuse; is it too late to stop doing drugs? No, obviously it isn't too late. You should stop as soon as possible. The sooner you stop the more time you have to work on getting rid of the habit. What happens if you slip up and go back to drugs of drinking? It will most likely happen. It doesn't have to happen but it can, you should expect to fall back a few times if you are addicted or have been doing it for a while. It isn't the end of the world just take it one day at a time. You should seek additional help if it's necessary.

Goodbye

Thanks for reading this book guys. I hope you learned something that you can take with you for the rest of your life. I hope if you've decided that you're life needs changes that you go through with them. If you really want to have the best relationship possible than you both need to focus on God and you're relationship should be about helping each other grow as Christians. I don't want you to think that I wrote this book to convert people, I didn't. I wrote this book to give people a chance at having the best relationship with their loved ones that they can. I wrote this book so that members of the opposite sex can learn to appreciate each other again.

But it's impossible for me to deny God. I've been completely honest with you up to this point and it'd be unfair if I stopped being honest at the end of my book. God gave me everything I know. He's the reason I'm a good boyfriend. If any of my advice was wise, than it was his wisdom, not mine.

So seriously, cultivate your love. Help it to grow, help it to flourish. Don't have less of a relationship than what's potentially possible. And try to weed out all of the foolishness and lies of this culture.

Go show your girlfriend (or boyfriend) some new love.

If you still have questions that need answers or are unsure of any material in this book or would simply appreciate advice concerning your relationship, feel free to contact me through Facebook. I should be under Keith Sobus.

NOTES

All bible verses used in this book come from BibleGateway.com and are from the New International Version (NIV) translation on their website.

Introduction

1. To learn more about Young Life and how you can get involved visit their official website at http://www.younglife.org/ I would strongly advise you to investigate it if it peaks your interest.

Modern Culture

1. Seventeen Magazine headlines were taken from Google images sometime in 2007
2. Cosmo Girl's website was also looked at sometime in 2007.

Love

1. Paraphrased from the song "Chasing Cars" by Snow Patrol. I'm not bashing the song, I actually really like it. I just happen to think that the lyrics of popular songs sometimes closely relate to the beliefs of the culture in which the song originates.

Pornography

1. http://internet-filter-review.toptenreviews.com/internet-pornography-statistics.html
2. http://internet-filter-review.toptenreviews.com/internet-pornography-statistics.html
3. http://internet-filterreview.toptenreviews.com/internet-pornography-statistics.html
4. http://internet-filter-reviews.toptenreviews.com/internet-pornography-statistics.html
5. http://64.233.169.104/search?q=cache:fI8oyBd41-MJ:www.womenofsubstance.org/por.htm+%22The+average+age+at+which+men +first+see+Playboy+or+a+similar+magazine+is +11%22&hl=en&ct=clnk&cd =1&gl=us&client=firefox-a

6. http://healthymind.com/s-porn-stats.html
7. http://healthymind.com/s-porn-stats.html
8. http://healthymind.com/s-porn-stats.html
9. http://healthymind.com/s-porn-stats.html
10. http://healthymind.com/s-porn-stats.html

Sex

1. http://legal-dictionary.thefreedictionary.com/impotent
2. http://www.fpv.org.au/1_10_10.html
3. http://www.harpers.org/subjects/Folly
4. http://www.indiana.edu/~owa/mjreport/98_aprmr.html
5. http://www.harpers.org/subjects/Sex
6. http://www.harpers.org/subjects/Marriage
7. http://www.kidzworld.com/article/1916-dear-dish-it-facts-about-sexually-active teens

Printed in the United States
205628BV00001B/38/P